MARY'S HOUSE

New and Selected Poems

by David Craig

Idylls Press
2007

First Edition from Idylls Press
April 2007

Idylls Press
P.O. Box 3566
Salem, OR 97302
www.idyllspress.com

Printed in the United States of America by Idylls Press

Cover photo and design by John Murphy

Library of Congress Cataloging-in-Publication Data

Craig, David, 1951-
  Mary's house : new and selected poems / by David Craig. -- 1st ed.
    p. cm.
  ISBN 978-1-59597-007-7 (alk. paper)
  I. Title.
  PS3553.R223M37 2007
  811'.54--dc22

Acknowledgements

Thanks to The Cleveland State University Poetry Center, White Eagle Coffee Store Press, Scripta Humanistica, and The Franciscan University of Steubenville Press, all of which published books or chapbooks containing many of these poems. I'd also like to thank journals which have accepted or published many of them: *American Literary Review, Ancient Paths, Bloomsbury Review, Burning Light, Caelum et Terra, The Catholic Exchange, Cha-Cha Review, The Christian Century, Christianity and Literature, The Cord, Cream City Review, Crux, First Things, The Formalist, Franciscan Way, Hiram Poetry Review, Image, A New Song, Rafale, Restoration, Silver Wings, Soundings, Spirituality & Health, Time of Singing, Wellspring,* and *Windhover.*

Thanks to Eastern University's Dr. Scott Robinson for putting "Lyrics" to his Christian Sufi music. His band is called *Mandala.* You can go to www.mandala.band.net and give him a listen.

And thanks to David Impastato for his *Upholding Mystery: An Anthology of Contemporary American Poetry* (Oxford University Press, 2002). "The Apprentice Eats Glass," "The Apprentice Sees Himself in the Sunset," "Nursing Home, 3rd shirt," "The Apprentice is Amazed," "The Apprentice Prophesies," "Our Father," "Hyperbole," and "Marian Sector" all appeared there, many in earlier forms.

David Craig
Weirton, WV
March, 2007

Table of Contents

SOME KIND OF PILGRIM (89)

Mary's House

New and Selected Poems

by David Craig

THE LEGEND OF THE THREE
COMPANIONS OF SAINT FRANCIS

Chapter I

His birth, vanity, frivolity, and prodigality; how he became generous and charitable to the poor.

Dignity underfoot, he turned his life
into a gabbling goose of a performance,
a wonking high wire poetic act,
him singing so loudly from stumps,
imaginary instruments, in horrible French,
that everyone who passed just had to watch
him dare himself, paint himself
into one spiritual corner after another,
until he had no options but severest Truth,
in the boisterous rhymes of the troubadours
set right, by a grin so local it owns the world.

It was his father who'd taken the first stride:
naming his son after a country
where they knew their fabric,
where they valued life's buckled and measured step
as well as its print—insisting on a carafe of friends,
ridiculous neighbors (though Pica, his mother,
had wanted the very breath of God: Giovanni!)

And so Francis learned to trade the prayer the best cloth was
for the smiles of new friends. After work,
his mates would ring in the chorus his money made:
a cascade of coins, grace,
surrounded as they all were,
by the cold stones of the only night.

It was all he could give them.

(Was he vain,
or just so caught up in his enthusiasms
that they'd begun to make their own demands?)

He'd sew rags to more expensive stuffs,
embracing, again, that widow: want,
knowing he could not, needing to tell everyone
that as well. So he became a jongleur,
a determined clown, standing in the breech
between the sorrowful truth of this world
and the fleeting faces of his friends.

So courteous in manner, speech,
even beyond his exaggerated, broadly beaming
self-conscious parody—everyone knew
he could name his own future.
He loved to pose, but only because it promised
what was, in some way, already here—

until a customer's smirk
blessed him, brought him down to squalor,
to a world beyond his making, to people with nothing to give
but their fleas.
    It was that wound again,
what he and all his friends felt:
the abyss which could not be filled
until now.

Given this cross, he wondered,
where could he live?

Chapter II

How he was imprisoned during Assisi's battle with Perugia and of the two visions he later had, wanting to become a knight.

He camped for his new peers,
as if he were that troubadour Bernart de Ventadorn,
fresh from the castle's bread kilns—
for the laughs he knew: dancing, skirt lifted
on cold stones, singing too loudly to birds
out the small window, telling rhymes
of fearful Assisian Knights.

Why *should* he worry? The world was new enough;
every morning everywhere mists came,
only to be burnt away by the sun,
so many new people around by afternoon,
no one could've guessed.

And so when the weight of the hours
began to take the measure of one knight's need
Francis would not back down.
He flanked the man, feinted, sang in bad langue d'oc
because he was a merchant's son:
"What do you think will become of me?
Rest assured, I will be worshiped
throughout the whole world."

Eventually released, a dream would wake him:
past the castles it offered, legions of runic and rubied arms—
which surpassed even his carefully chosen own;
offered shields: walled fields of them, bronzing sunlight.

Chivalry so moved in him the next morning
that he gave all his clatter away.
Friends laughed, wondered if his stirruped feet
were (ever) on the ground.
But Francis, for his part, he figured, yes,
yes, he could give them this;
he could show them the answer that was possible
before its time, be its fool, its peacock,
anything to help them see.

When asked the reason for his glow, Francis
answered largely, as if he were one:
"I shall become a great prince."
Why else were dreams given, but to make us princes
(and holy fools) before we would become one
(preparing him to turn the world upside down)?

He wondered, what would be asked of him?
How could he be a princely knight
and wear the holy ribbons of Mother Church too?
And what of his lady-who-must-be-in-waiting?

Morning came, and Francis,
sitting on a stump, rejoiced,
kept that marvelous engine, his future,
as best he could,
stabled in his junket-heart.

Chapter III

How the Lord visited Francis' heart for the first time, filling it with marvelous tenderness that gave him strength to begin to progress spiritually in looking down on himself and all vanities, in prayer, almsgiving and poverty.

A party for the new money, and more,
from the very stems of delight: ladies—
each of his pals, now enjoying
what was left of the tipsy night, some steps in front of him,
their misplaced lives, as ever, just out of reach.

Francis, ever the jester, chose to walk behind,
scepter in his hand, dressed as he was,
in silks and tatters, knowing by now that rags
really were riches, either way:
metaphor for the chase,
the shell games of wealth and fame;
for that, or for the more quiet, obvious need.

But how could he get his friends
to know what was real, and missing,
what demanded so much?

They came back to him, their captain in mirth
elsewhere, looking up, seemingly lost
in the glorious conflagration of stars.

Was he contemplating the crimson stomacher?

"Yes, you are right!" he answered.
"And I shall take a wife—more noble, wealthy,
and beautiful than any you have never seen."

But they didn't laugh when he said, "Poverty...
the one we all chase without knowing it..."

And after that day, he never denied an alms
to anyone who asked
in God's only name. Heaping his absent father's table
with begged bread, Francis piled his want high
in joyful exasperation,
(in front of his grieving mother:
that the world would, so soon,
begin hammering away
at his white-hot enthusiasms,
bend him—all out of shape).

But Francis was, as ever, elsewhere:
and pressing his face between Rome's bars,
he tossed his last flightless bird, bag of coins,
high and crashing down onto Peter's tomb.

Needing to try on his life,
he swapped clothes with a beggar.

Yes! Yes! These would help him keep himself
in a line, would help him keep the world far away,
with its trumpets, bandied names!
This way he'd never confuse himself again.
He'd wake up next to new brothers: lepers,
dew on his rags, soiled feet.
He sang loudly, played fiddlesticks
on the open road, so that the world
would be forced to mark him,
hold him to what mattered.

Once back, he didn't share his secret,
because he was betrothed to a lady, Poverty,
a woman hidden in so much beauty
that a look from anyone at all
would have violated, surely, their first
intimate steps.

Chapter IV

How he began to overcome himself by his dealing with lepers.

Praying loudly, so that God would mark him mark
the degree of his need,
Francis was given every ragged thing,
told to wrap each in the fish paper, soiled strings
of his cloistered heart.

And so, coercing his distant, perfect mouth,
Francis made himself kiss what was left
of the leper's hand, helped fold it,
cracking, crackling over the scarred coins
he'd managed to lodge there.
And the diseased cloth of lip, hot rasp of peace
returned, marked Francis's face
with all that was rank and alive,
squirming inside him.

He joined them finally, a leper
before he became one: these men marked
with strength enough to bear the inside of the cup;
he kissed what he could find, hold of every hand,
face, pressed each to the clear water
of his cheeks, giving them
the waste that was his life, his years.

In earnest repetition, he found what he needed there:
the swollen face of God, in every dropsy eye,
crusted smile. And because he finally learned
to embrace that gift, he had to endure the next:
departure, toward those more obviously afflicted.

The devil made after him, but Francis felt too poor
to be considered so. His life, after all,
had been, up until that second, was still,
one long stain of need.

He tore his clothes, would continue to do as much,
but how could he walk now, whose step could he use?

Chapter V

How the crucifix spoke to him for the first time and how he henceforth carried the passion of Christ in his heart until death.

The corpus moved
like huge, dark stones inside him.
It was his future, yes—death,
but it was the rut in the land too,
the stag's opened throat; the sin in every merchant
coin: a flood of offenses—years before his own skin
would yaw, open.

Outside the Portiuncula, he cried out—
because no one ever did,
because the world would not.

He would make it his rooftop then,
shout in a loud voice to wake the forest,
all the unfruitful dead beyond.

He'd sprinkled chaste "Brother Ash" on his food
because we never think to do the same.

And because Mary had to scrounge,
he rushed to the ground, ate with the pigs
at his brothers' feet—.
If they couldn't see how crucial humility was,
how would anyone else?

He'd stop so often, lost in loud sighs:
his aloneness, their burden;
he'd provoke, disrupt them

out of any earned rest, meal.
He'd tell them that when they heard the next sigh,
they should praise God for His great condescension;
they should pray for Francis continually,
whose need was at least as great as their own.

⚜

Poems Based on the
Stigmata Section of
The Fioretti

St. Francis received the wounds of Christ on Mount Alvernia in Italy, in 1224. The events surrounding the miraculous wounding and the stigmata itself are recorded in the pasticcio that is the oral tradition in "The Little Flowers of Saint Francis." The following poems are meditations based on those recorded events. Hopefully they catch something of the spirit they are meant to embody, something of that tradition.

In the first poem Francis meets and helps to convert a wealthy man who offers him the gift of a mountain. In the second, Francis occupies it, praying, when a devil comes to tempt him—and as we learn, some decades later, another brother is tried in the same place. After his encounter, Francis, feeling even more acutely the disease that is eating at his bones, prepares for his death. An angel comes to comfort him. And in the third poem, after Leo catches Francis in an ecstasy, the angel appears again, this time to warn Francis to prepare for a special favor. Jesus Himself then appears in the form of a six-winged seraph, gives the Little One the stigmata. The whole valley lights up as Francis is told he will be allowed to go down to purgatory on his feast day every year to bring back any of his faithful. At end, Francis offers his pierced hands to his brothers.

⚜

I. The First Consideration of the Holy Stigmata
(The Mountain is Offered)

In the forty-third year of his Lord,
this little man, bread for the birds,
set off. (Like us, but without
our sense of direction.)
Oblivious, in a place
where flowers spoke:
the tongues of God,
green-throated,
in petals, pistil.

On they would walk,
him so sunk in his robe
that you had to go through the smiles
to find him—
earth, a place to be swept,
cleaned: broom of dirt
on a sea of dirt,
dirt on dirt dancing.

He wanted to be a dandelion spore,
tiny piked pinwheel,
silk with a snag,
under the great wooden
cart-like wheel of the stars.

The monied Orlando de Chiuse,
wanted his heart rings numbered;
he wanted to hear
what these tatters had wrought—
the years having pushed
the best years away.

He saw and detested it:
this self, this house of cards,
shill under ornate glass—
a topography of Lent,
the burden of strong men:
a collection plate
feeding more hands.

"So great is the good I hope for,
all pain delights me..."

(This was a different time
I should tell you.
People listened. And each,
in his own hearing,
received the measure
of his pain: smaller
than the wound at Jesus' side,
stretch and serous fluid,
His quiet breathing:
the catch in his ribs—
steps, like uneven playing field,
each of your friends,
one by one, leaving;
just you in snake-skin boots,
off the Trailways
at the edge of this no-town—
the abandoned gas station,
ancient, rusty shell-white
pumps, the hot crackle
of tall, dry grass,
the sting of grasshoppers
as you walk through a field,
duffle bag in hand.

And finally, as you expected,
the distant gathering of skyline,
your life, dark,
across the southern
Colorado plain:

the throat of God.)

Orlando wanted out,
of himself, what that was,
away from the easy laughter
of tenant friends.

Yes, "most willingly," Francis
would speak to him.
"But first honor thy friends
who have invited thee to feast."
(All things in time,
at time's pace, so that time
and earth might be valued.)

And then the mountain
offered: but this gift, like Francis,
would not be about him.
And so, soldiers in tow,
the blazing began,
                on one side:
a line of shaven heads,
measuring prayer,
a few of the wayward
on the periphery,
where the only voice
they wanted to hear was "God's":
in green leaf, the drinking

of water against sunny banks,
right through to refracted feet—
how it thirsted one, for the Spirit
and for how *He* meant things;
not the sound of ruin, military feet—
                    and on the other:
aching feet in issued boots,
the company swill that grumbled
long before rations.

Everyone there beginning
in that place everyone does,
out of the place
he had settled on:
the glamourless gospel,
accomplished through repetition,
the showing up.
(The time beneath time
were time noun enough.
Grace and movement,
and it's the effort that stays:
the long and quiet patience of God.)

Eventually, Masseo de Marignano,
Angelo Tancredi, and Leo, the slow,
go with him: James, Peter, John;
they watched him ascend.
This was just one more place
they could not go: the slow patrol,
the troop with too many voices.
Like us, they knew half the way there:
the hand half-outstretched,
the smile plainly given.

When he came down
in strength not his own,
the brothers got him an ass:
a different one—an owner
with something to say.
"Be nothing
less than people
hope of thee."

Sitting at the foot of the mountain,
ridiculous as the pigeons
on his head, his legs, a bird dropping
on his robe, Francis smiled,
his back against a tree.
"God is pleased," he said,
"because so much joy is shown
by our sisters and brothers, the birds."

Men rolled to their feet,
followed him,
quiet as a suburban lawn
any morning.

II. The Second Consideration of the Holy Stigmata
(Preparation)

Orlando heaped up food
to crowd the hermit's appetite,
wine to wet the failing eye.
And Francis, having been fathered himself,
opened under that green canopy:
clouds, laughter,
the singing of rain on leaves.
He thought of his own happiness,
all the nights back when,
when stars or clouds
were his great company.

After Orlando's visit
he went back to towering beeches.
Once more God's soft, leafy hands,
and only death now between them,
the garden stretching skyward:
there before the moon was moon,
cooled as it was,
in an egress of geese.

He knew what his brothers
needed from him,
that he see who he was.

The next day, he walked great fissures,
mountain: symbol for the congealed,
us, who, for want of praise,
find ourselves split, other.
Brothers watched him rise,
bring back their thoughts, sin.

Many chose, not surprisingly,
wider orbits;
around him, themselves.

Francis' only steady company
was a consoling angel:
the order stays,
the order stays;
even the foulest, if he love the order,
mercy; those who persecute
with malice: short life—
a laundry list for the pure of heart.

Many will be perfect.

Encouraging his want,
Francis fasted on the Assumption,
meditating on a life where,
after the angel,
the only voice she probably heard
was her own laundry.
And now these little tramps:
Francis, who, running
Chaplinesque Leo back and forth
to much mountain shouting,
finally found a place
where no one could hear him,
inspect.

In silence, he would be elsewhere:
a healthy fool made to lie down
and lose what he had grown to love:
his little life, spooned out
of his mouth for his kin,

lifted up like the joyful paralytic,
back through the roof of heaven.

And because he was so small,
the devil came: some abomination
of nature, leaved, licking the hunch
on its back, seeking to tear him apart;
but Francis held to rocks
which became wax,
veiled him.

Doubled, losing in the losing,
our sorry friend
humped and hunkered away
like a sputtering machine
clamped to its nut,
without savor, sinking deeper
into that desperate glee,
where the only thing to enjoy
is self humoring self,
audience of one,
returns diminishing.

And that same limp, decades later,
shook a friar between his teeth,
spat him down,
the brother crying out as he fell,
log bridge on his head.

In an instant, Francis
set him down, completed,
at the bottom.
Meanwhile, his brothers,
who had heard the voice,

came for the body, were amazed—.
They found it, singing,
log still on his head.

What could they do?
They sang as well: the bottom
of this chasm, some with clumps
of dirt on their heads,
some arm in arm,
each looking foolish enough
to stick out.

Because he was no leader
they came, because he never knew
what to say.

This time it was a bird,
who would be the one to remind him
just how much he needed.
It would wake him for matins,
singing or beating its wings.
He'd rise, crack his knuckles,
or not when his bones
refused the call,
the cold giving-way in them,
when he could feel each move
toward parchment:
hollow and gaunt, hungry
as his feasting self.

It would sit with him,
push pebbles around
to his fingers in the dirt.

III. The Third Consideration of the Holy Stigmata (Gifts)

Yellow-faced in the torch
descending, Leo saw it rest
on the unkempt head,
an absent voice
murmuring in the shake and gilt
of late summer leaves.

Turning, disobedient, to go,
he heard his rescue.
At forgiveness' still whole feet,
he wept. And Francis,
what could he give his charge
beyond a playful tug on Leo's ear,
all of his own?

Yes, God *would do* holy things
on this mountain.
All the world will wonder.
(Leo wondered.)

Together they opened the Bible,
to the Passion,
and Francis felt it again:
in fleet gray clouds,
hulking trees,
in the roads and rocks.
He knew that God was the One
who still rose in the stars
every night, the One
who coddled him

in the breath and muzzle
of cold night skies.

And the repaying?
This small, sad life given,
though he knew
it couldn't be little enough.

And so, heavy, on the spool
of his nature,
Francis turned east, like the Soldan,
begged again for one last grace:
(as God had reckoned all his time,
One's delight being the other's Joy),
to feel the passion bodily,
where it was real, in the fiber
of heart muscle,
in tendons, the road, dolorosa,
beneath his feet.

And so God inflamed him
upward, drew him
to the six-winged Seraph, Himself,
a Soul to meet his own:
that surest Sun,
moving steadily—
on the cross, crucified;
two of the wings extended
above His head:
the Father, as ever, being glorified;
two wings, below, outstretched,
to still the world;
and the last two,
drawing them together:

this return for Francis only—
him now so lost
in the bright cloud
and twiggy stuff of feathers,
that he missed his own convulsings:
the groans, spasms,
his side searing
without blood,
and then the flesh opening:
his entrails in sunlight.

Francis had seen the truth—
and had the sense
to just stand there,
lighting up the whole left side
of the mountain.

Shepherds saw it for an hour,
wondered, looked for wise men, a king.
Perhaps one had decreed it day,
a tax on all who resisted?
Silk or the mud they were in?

Hostelry windows, too, blinked,
so early, it seemed, this rising;
yawns in creaking beds,
the maid turning up and out,
butter churn in hand,
cold as the months to come.

And certain muleteers
who were going to Romagna,
believing that the first light

had come from the rising sun,
saw it cease.

When the natural sun rose,
one of them suggested two days' pay.

And in that second light Giovanni
promised an anniversary:
on his death date to descend,
God's breath, out over pale waters,
into Purgatory, to deliver
even, perhaps, us—
a sign, what Jesus would do
for the least of these.

(And who, now,
would notice him come down,
this kiss of Christ, dirt and wounds
to any ruby-crowned,
fully-fleshed head?)

Red lines of pain mapped the force
and reel of Francis's blood
in open air.

He'd hold them, his hands on his lap
like a couple of dying birds,
quailing, or behind his back,
fingers that couldn't grip,
gripping fingers.

Leo had to tear the cloth off,
away from his hands, side,
beneath the piercing cries of heaven.

Francis left the mountain
to his friends. Where he was going,
they could not follow, yet,
as Jesus told Peter.

And finally, with Leo beside him,
he rode back to St. Mary of the Angels.
He gave his hands to his brothers
to touch and kiss, the pain of living,
an opened wound, the heart of God,
its slow beat and decline.

He wanted to die on common dirt,
to feel the good cold ground
seep into the dust that was his flesh.
He wanted to feel it take him in.

Poems based on St. Thérèse's Last Conversations

—As recorded by her sister, Mother Agnes

The spirituality of St. Thérèse is one of "spiritual childhood"; that is, she remained "little," entirely dependent upon God the Father for her every need, completely confident in His generous good will regarding her life. She had St. Paul's ambition for spiritual things, wanted to be all things in the Church, its heart finally, and perhaps because of this, she is singularly honored among Catholics. Using these deathbed conversations as starting points, I have tried to come to grips with that sensibility.

April 7

"Allowing her to see my fears, I asked her what sort of death
I would die. She answered with a very tender smile: 'God
will sip you up like a little drop of dew.'"

And she was right.
Mother Agnes, fifty-four revolutions later—
first the coma, was sipped, as if the taste
demanded pause: the long, quiet life
given, like each of ours,
gathered for a final draw.

She loved as one always must,
in silence.

Dorothy Day called it the long loneliness,
the wine glass lifted; small puddles,
the wet shake of birds beneath wind
and a shifting rain from trees, tall grass
running along the convent wall.
The speed of gray clouds,
how they become our lives,
all the beauty here; we feel
what we cannot hold, only contain.
It's the God we cannot have:
leaving, staying.

What courage it takes to live here!
Anything given
in a world running like clouds.

May 1

*"My heart was filled entirely with a heavenly peace today. I
prayed much to the Blessed Virgin last night, thinking that
her beautiful month was about to begin!"*

The leaves, finally, assert themselves,
and the sun, no stranger in the sky.

Who doesn't stretch out to his full height today?
Who doesn't walk the wooded paths
amid the chatter of green companions?

Even the slug, under a lifted rock, circles,
exhilarated, and the stream, like some young colt,
noses in the water.
The day, so clearly fastened between ground and sky,
is a call to someplace where we'll feel the grass grow
through our skin as we recline,
where the sky will move
like the muscles in our faces.

May 15

> *"I am very happy to go to heaven very soon, but when I think*
> *of these words of God: 'My reward is with me, to render to*
> *each according to his works,' I tell myself that He will be very*
> *much embarrassed in my case. I haven't any works! Well,*
> *then. He will reward me 'according to His own works.'"*

Here is perfect commerce: the opened palm.
Here, no sense of industry,
only the movement of intersection:
our works, hers. We are made new
in old skins.

Thérèse, little post in the ground,
evidence that there is no Texas, California,
Harvard here.

These transparent saints!
No wonder they come so quickly, moving
leaves in all these trees! They become us,
our breathing, the days we live in.

And at sunset, these same ones
walk the beach, collecting alms: works.
They offer graying waters,
whatever shoes we have on.

May 21-26

"After my death, I don't want to be surrounded with wreaths or flowers as Mother Genevieve was. To those who want to give these, you will say that I would rather they spend this money in the ransom of little black babies. This will please me."

Sunken cheeks on network news,
the always, it seems, brown eyes:
mother of all looks, who we are
made clear in the eyes of the dying.

This is what our lives are like
on spring days, when everything sings,
lost in green song. These are
the happy birds, here, and there,
the nice houses. And out on a great lake,
it will kill you, white lace
on the breeze-tossed waves.

The beauty, its passing;
our hearts, like our smiles,
so easy to change!

May 27 Ascension

> *"I always see the good side of things. There are some who
> set about giving themselves the most trouble. For me, it's
> just the opposite. If I have nothing but pure suffering, if the
> heavens are so black that I see no break in the clouds, well,
> I make this my joy! I revel in it!"*

God's goodness is His own.
It's a child delighting in rain.
It's the intellect working
within a larger clock.

"If they see me as stupid, very well;
there is much I do not know."

But who else holds the lake in her palm,
who else struts upon its plant-like stem?
Wheat teacher, read us again;
we want to run through the vales of your voice:
the French hillside, slate sky, swirls of birds.

Children hear the bell, come in.
The grasses begin to dim, shouts gradually
eaten by the darkening trees. The barn,
too, dims, settles like the head
of the family dog.

Aristotle, Terence, come in too.
We are tired and have been waiting for you.

Will the posing never end?
Will the learned ever put away their begging cups?

What do you know worth keeping, wise man?
If it were worth anything, wouldn't you give it away?

May 27 Ascension

"Did you notice during the reading in the refectory, the letter
addressed to the mother of St. Louis de Gonzague, in which
it said…that had he lived to the age of Noah he would not
have learned more or become more holy? She said this because
of some remarks that were made about the necessity of a long
life in the service of God."

Merits for most of us pile
like duty logged: a drowned carcass,
a wooden leg. Which is why
she is all eye, a blink on a bed,
seeing clearly, tender as any morning.

This woman in her lens,
caught in the webs of a busy mind,
her self, so many explosions,
the East Coast and the fish are dying.

What did you want?
A bigger bushel, more pears?
Were you going to build a house here?

The beauty is in the passing,
the aging face, the trees that will
outlast us, friends gone so far from us
that they don't want the pain
lost years would bring. Bad choices,
potential that might've been there.
But this is what makes them worth seeking:
old campaigners, the wizened faces,
the moving through: steady mules.

May 29

" 'Pointes de feu' applied for the second time in the evening. I was sad, and seeking consolation, opened the Gospels in her presence. My eyes fell upon these words: 'He is risen: He is not here; see the place where they laid Him.' "

"Yes, that's really true! I am no longer, in fact, as I was in my childhood, open to every sorrow; I am as one risen; I am no longer in the place where they think I am."

God's will was sweet,
it was all she had of Him:
each moment, His calm hands
wrapped around the chalice of her own.
Yes was always the place.
Now, always the price.
And when her breath became short,
a hundred quick doors closing,
could that be any different?

Every life ends, every death
rehearsed, and each one,
a movement toward a further
opening of a flower,
the whole self seeking release:
a symphony of praise,
in the angled run of a dog,
in a small convent,
in the corner of France.

June 4

"A little later, being alone with her, and seeing her suffer very much, I said: 'Well, you wanted to suffer, and God hasn't for- gotten it.'"

Death, our little pal with the big teeth,
like the piranha my friend has mounted
in his kitchen: each tooth, an incisor,
each fishy happy enough to hang
like a Japanese lantern from your side,
leaving you bone and the river.
And the river won't mind, one more undulation,
the joy in the noise it will find itself making.
Your bones, half-submerged, will shine, white
in the sun. You will be like the man
in the white hat, and the sun will ache
to have such playmates. White on white,
the two of you will wash the scene in light.
Maybe a native will canoe by, see you there.
He will look for a moment, move on.
You will have had your spree.
More time will come and take you;
you will collapse in a heap, meet more of the river.

Who could give this? The arch of her back,
the voice she kept inside her, silent,
like a field of headless chickens,
their inarticulate bobbings. How slowly
they lie down, the only noise the sound
their feet make, stepping dumbly over each other,
the occasional flap of wing.

All of this would be absurd if you were not of it,
if you did not arch a little bit in their going.

This is what she gave, the untuning.
You are there, too, if you read this.
Welcome to the provinces, where you are the sleek curve
and spitting sound through water whales make,
their shiny eel-like move as they submerge.
This is us again: into sunlight, back to grief.
One, our home, the other, our story.
We fish here, Mr. and Mrs. Janus,
a group called the Optics.
Grab a net, feel the rock in the boat.

June 5

"I have read over again the play Joan of Arc that I composed. You will see there my sentiments on death; they are all expressed; this will please you. But don't believe I'm like Joan of Arc when she was afraid for a moment.... She was tearing her hair out!...I myself am not tearing out my 'little' hair."

Young nun suited, photographed,
a stanchion in the cold
of convent quiet, in the dew
morning makes on steel.

Aligning herself with the peonies,
she would fight the battle of the grasses.
Roseate dawns she could never see
past. She answered a call
that was her skin,
sought every irritation,
oddity thrust at her in a black bustle:
arms crabbing, neurotic knots of energy,
whatever battle going on,
fought too close to the surface, for all of us.

That much was clear,
so she went there every time,
the nurse who suffered because she was the patient.
The agony that comes with this fleshy dress,
so beautiful, that each time,
it has only one face.

Anna-Maria Taigi:
The Preparation

"Quantitative judgments do not apply."
—Gervais Crouchback

The scandal is not that Jesus matters; it's that, in
the end, He is the only thing that matters.

*Anna-Maria Taigi was a hearty peasant woman who lived in
Rome during the French Revolution and the subsequent Bonaparte
regime. Like most European Catholics, she watched with shock and
amazement as both Pius VI and Pius VII were abused in turn by
the invaders. But, strangely, she may well have been a participant
here too, as God apparently granted her a most unusual favor: For
forty-seven years, it has been reported in the Process, she could see
through a globe, which became visible to her, actual events as they
occurred in the world. She could participate in a spiritual manner:
pray for and suffer with people. If so, why had God done this? Who
could say for sure? Perhaps to provide a kind of communications
satellite for the ragged remains of the Catholic Church in Rome,
the Cardinals she knew there; or perhaps, again, to remind us that
surface players, presidents or statesmen, no matter how powerful,
are in the end only that. This poem attempts to trace the beginnings
of what had to have been a very unique call.*

White Noise

Under an accumulation of stones, the press
of histories, scat-tered voices,
in-house glossolalias,
she no doubt heard each new take,
each rhetorician convinced
that beneath his discourse lurked life,
each with a soul now to prove it.
Like old Voltaire, who,
according to the Curé of Ars, couldn't,
despite his late and shaded voicings,
get a death-bed pardon, or Minister Choiseul,
peddling *The Encyclopedia*, a kind of symphony
which excluded the Jesuits, they were hawkers,
like all of us, at the Noise Café:
Louis XV or any president on his stage
of history, the attendant puppets
who want to pull their own strings:
Mme. du Barry or the Pompadour before.

The twelve hundred Parisians who scattered,
panicked by fireworks, were metaphor—
each person running from failed design,
yellow umbrellas of light,
red glare rockets singeing the grass,
scattered masses trying to get free
while the larger planetary bop, all but clouded
by the sput and fizzle of the times,
busied itself in the backdrop of their lives.
Whether we sit or stand, they,
the fuel of our scorn, are us, mercenaries
in the war against faith, right reason.

Unschooled in truth, history,
we beat our own drums, get lost
in the echoes, in the less than perfect thunder
of our lives, the almost original notes
we register, carry in tubas, (muffled praise, denials)
over chalked white lawns, half-time stadia turf.

The Vision that Directs Us

Born in Siena, two months before Napoleon,
she would keep her jump on him:
thirty years later, their souls, like rosebushes,
trellising the chair of Peter;
he, a prince to his own coming,
she, a doorkeeper's wife.
The two of them in a tug of war over Pius VII,
who would be dragged from prison to drugs
in exchange for a fleetless Emperor's promise:
pension money.
            And Napoleon?
Mercy would send him a jailer,
an October letter from the Vicar
urging ease for the man
who had brought religion back to France.

It's the invertedness of the whole affair
that fascinates, peasants moving the cosmic dance,
kings and Popes, all of history, apart from us
in the end, written by characters
we've hardly heard of, in a choreography
across time we never see.

Take Catherine, for instance,
who preceded her, who, at six,
from the wide lap of her mother,
had seen Jesus' eyes grace the domed skull
of San Domenico—where now her own head
teaches, begins to darken in this state.
Dressed in pontificals, He asked her
to tether Peter's bark,
seventy-four years afloat on strange waters.

One peasant and then another,
beyond the pages men would write,
separated by centuries, connected as we all are,
on a stage much larger than the vision
which directs us: Anna, who at six, too, turned,
before an accusing sun
in self-conscious clothes,
old packages, strings to tie up their lives,
her father's business failure
following them out of town.

It was 1775, and Pius VI, who was to die
a prisoner at Valance, half-paralyzed,
having been driven first over the Apennines,
then the Alps in his eighties,
his dead body finally getting the pomp
it so enjoyed, used late by Napoleon
in an attempt to sway the College of Cardinals,
had declared *this* a Holy Year.

The girl watched her father stop,
shift the weight of their load,
grunt against the times;
they put up nights under farmhouse faces,
each one, charitable to them
in its measuring degree.

She smoothed the big wheel,
once, watched the stars overhead;
the rhythmic squeaking moving her
to take those first sure steps outside of time,

the currents of events,
marking the road as her home.

She never understood much
but from where she was,
reading the tea leaves of faces, the night now
in the hard shoulders of her father
as he bent ever forward, pushing, like the horses,
toward the stone face of eternity.

Family

They wedged into dei Monti,
where St. Benedict Labré, "the beggar of Rome,"
who had finally stopped walking, lived.
He'd met the Curé's father on his way there
years before—his flea-bitten pilgrimage
now ending where it had always been conducted,
on cathedral steps, this time
near a young girl who would help another beggar,
the Church, through times which wanted its end.

And for Benedict: no order could refuse him now,
patron of transients, the housed.
He who had known the value of his flesh,
crucified, was carried into a butcher's shop
in the Via dei Serpenti, died there,
each second of his thirst, an attentive response
through and in this market for our skins.

Santa, Anna's mother, a charwoman,
like Vianney, senior, earlier perhaps,
held the sainted moment for her memory,
washing hardening limbs,
combing the hair, part of her
wanting to assume the whole relic,
locket it in the cool, dark tomb of her heart.
She wanted to live with it there,
walk again under a blue sky: a clear bell—.

But within the borders of the free school,
her daughter, waiting perhaps for her final form,
may have delighted instead
in the audible play of dresses.

Perhaps she gave imaginative room
to make-overs, bouffants, to gathered petticoats,
bum rolls, to pom-poms she'd heard,
sewn to the back waistline, one's hair, deshabille.
Maybe she wore a mobcap, a tube skirt
with Ionic fastenings in her dreams.

But if she did, that vanity didn't last.
Grace would have her—
as it will have, if we are blessed, us:
her roots finally finding their appointed soil
in the veins of her mothers,
as she learned how to make a good stock,
wind and warp silk, until the pox
traced our mortal way through her still striking face,
taking her from school before she'd learned
to comfortably write her name,
the scars reminding her
that you can never come back
from where you never leave.

She found her joy in the smells of her father's house,
dug in her heels, just to hear the good
and meaningful crunch of dirt:
one more holy peasant on a yoke of land,
giving more than she could know, each "yes,"
like the many before, answering entire armies,
which turn the soil, again and again,
old bones over old bones.
And like the saints before her,
she helped lift Napoleon, perhaps,
on his deathbed to receive,
or farther down the corridors of time:

a Native American Iwo Jima vet who would die,
drunk in a shallow puddle; pietas both,
each place made real for the first time,
by the hammer, nails, that sound
which echoes down the systolic and sacred chambers
of a beating Human Heart.

Stages

In France at this time, Necker was dancing
as fast as he could, trying to save Louis' show,
Beaumarchais doing the same for rebel America,
profits care of his play, *Figaro*.
Meanwhile, Diderot, who had been tonsured at thirteen,
written missionary tracts
to assuage a Jansenist conscience,
and who soon would be canonized
in his own library by Catherine of Russia,
was publishing "tolerance," "sexual liberty."
Friedrich Anton Mesmer, his ear tuned
to the vibes of the stars, might have heard a phrase
of percussive truth, but he was convinced
that convulsions could restore
the natural flow of universal fluids.

Anna, though, knew what she was
apart from her Lord, and so sat quietly,
allowing His mice to gnaw their slow story
along the woodwork of her soul,
as she handled silk in a cold dress shop,
felt the pull of sentimental novels.

And in March, 1782, the world,
on the stage of time, intervened:
her parish priest, like some voice out of *Revelations*,
begged from the pulpit for the two-headed
prince of Christendom:
Pius VI and Franz Joseph.
He prayed for sacramentalism, confraternities,
as the collar of the times tightened,
as the Church paid the price for owning.

And when Pius returned to his See of enthusiastic
pre-dawn disciples, Anna was there, too,
could read the lines on his face, feel the man
sink in those creases, like death,
beneath what and where it could not settle:
the tribulations of a compassionate father
about to begin for both of them.

And so she responded, became a holy sign,
an absence signified, in hiddenness,
a bright wound of praise to move out,
smooth whatever had left its fold:
the rank and stumbling bleat of talkers,
sheep like whims in every direction.

She housled a limp, a joy that *was* laughter—
so deep-bellied that it found its form in wide skies,
running water, this life and the road that eats, golden,
us, her arms raised like green trees
she could live under.

Monied Vienna, meanwhile,
which had always known better,
was too busy to look back from her plow.
On the heels of a gayer Paris,
she snapped up any sharp, patterned movement
of feet. Temptations older than any of us
as we waltz with the spiritual life we know
because, arm in arm, we've brought her,
wearing the red dress we like,
filling our ears with what we know of love.

A Place for the Birds

In 1787, her father, on the lucky side
of all those learned tracts,
found enough to keep him indebted,
at the heels, in audience for the rich:
service at the Maccarani palace—
where Anne was saved by a better,
who, as a sign of his almost native French worth,
offended her with a few cultured asides:
ennui, apparently, being beyond her big feet,
potato ways.

(The Curé, in Ars, would soon be boiling
three days' worth at a time.)

And then, as if on heavenly cue,
Dominico appeared, robust as the rose
in a good dark wine, at twice the height.
He was roughly cut, full of himself, opinions.
But pious, too, looking at brisk home
in a serving coat, wide-shouldered:
a wild ass of a man really, one who valued work,
his loud pulse as it tested his neck's arterial walls.

(Before it had lost its wealth,
the Taeggi valley had been made straight
by mountains of fifteenth century timber;
Count Palantine Taeggi, founder of a college at Milan,
having cemented the bricks to his name,
would've been appalled to find it gutted
for the saint by the good nuns

who misspelled it on her daughters' schoolbooks:
a monastic mistake, a sign of His nameless hidden
who breathe well
beneath the trees of self-promotion.)

When he saw her, twenty, did birds fly up
across the square, accompanied by strings?
Were the ripples in nearby rivers shaken to the oars
that manned them? Maybe.
But he needed a wife too.
A union was worked out along the edges
of their busy lives. "My Mother," daughter Sophie said,
"did not want to be forever at home
warming the seat."
Bouquets of white roses were a movement
past the unvarnished life of the poor.
If a future was theirs to fashion,
she probably wanted to get her hands into the dough of it.
Delays could only bring distractions, temptations to dally.

> *I want there to be tin whistles,*
> *drums. I want there to be peasants feasting,*
> *Brueghel-like dancing; I want feet stomping*
> *because they finally could,*
> *the laughter of old warriors: the women,*
> *but men too, arm over arm,*
> *drinking out of any bottle in the open air,*
> *under a cadenza of moving stars,*
> *the breeze, eyes wet enough*
> *to make those heavenly voices flicker,*
> *chill the mortal bone; just enough of it*
> *to whole-heartedly recommend the present.*

It's not hard to imagine Anna,
both her arms muffing her husband's
as they strolled at their new pace through the squares.
Though poor, he may have bought her red to wear.
And if, at times, she found herself
walking once more through school day fabrics,
enjoying the kind looks of old strangers,
who could blame her, warm as she must have been
in the first flush of marriage?

The Second Oldest Song

Inside the palace "of three hundred windows,"
in what looked like, with its cast-iron discalced gratings,
brick walls, a convent, she must've felt
like she was moving through Eden,
what might have been in minuet:
open-armed staircases of swirling white marble,
mannered rooms in gold brocade—
like the fine talk of traveled people.
There were statues smooth and white as milk,
purple and orange tapestries,
iron-clad warriors on landings,
and high above, a vault for angels.

The servants' quarters were, not surprisingly,
something less: two squatting rooms
opposite the Colonna Square,
along a trough of alley called "Sdrucciolo,"
(the Slope), hemmed in as they were
between large-petalled flowers, mansions.
Rivulets of waste ran down her street,
reminding the poor of their surest angel.

And by 1790, elsewhere, he *had* checked in:
the French National Assembly
had taken to calling itself "Constituent,"
reinvented the rights of man.
By January 21 of that year,
Dr. Gullotin had proposed the first painless shave.
By February 13, the foundation and scaffolding of society,
the contemplative, had been banned.
And, as if to celebrate, on the 14th, in Rédon,
angry peasants set fire to an Abbey.

By April, church property went up for sale,
Robespierre calling for married priests.

"God inspires members of the Constituent Assembly,"
cried Dom Gerle, a Carthusian-about-town,
on June 13th, as he quoted the saintly Suzette Labrousse,
whose cause he trumpeted with indisputable facts:
eleven years before she had prophesied
that the clergy would lose their wealth,
the Pope, temporal power. And miracles!
When she was young she'd spread quicklime on her face
to avoid the temptation of the flesh,
but because that was not God's way,
her face bloomed, a lily, white as truth.

By July 12th, priests, bishops are to be democrats,
serve as a dissonant chorus for the Church of France.
On the 14th, a festival of the Federation
is held on Paris' Champ de Mars,
with an altar to a notion at the center:
three hundred thousand harriers, circling the insubstantial,
a ripple of collected pages.

By November, priests must swear allegiance
as theatrical productions echo progress.
In March of '91 *Cloistered Victims* plays at the République:
a heroine, locked up in a convent
is forced by the resident priest to sign over property.
After the initial performance, a patron, emboldened,
like someone from "Oprah," rises up,
admits that he, too, had been forced to become a monk,
learn repentance.

In April, marketplace women at the Filles de Sainte Marie,
begin to range from convent to convent,
looking for skirted priests.
Some porters are beaten, left bleeding in the snow.
And within six months, the hunt is on:
in July two priests are murdered at Bordeaux,
one the Vicar General Langorian,
and in September, one hundred fourteen priests soak the
                                garden of Carmes.
Set upon, their heads are split open like melons,
each sent to his great reward, piked,
wriggling, like a large worm in the dirt
until there wasn't enough body left alive
to come back to.

She saw, suffered no doubt as spiritual midwife
for some of the fifty thousand who were put in prison, killed.
Pius VII, raising Peter's voice from the grave
each time, speaking the Truth
that the world never quite hears,
nor more irritatingly, can ever be rid of.

Coming to Terms

Pearls on Domenico's arm,
her reverie is broken by Father Angelo,
who hears: "Her...I have chosen her to be a saint."
The priest stares intently into Anna's eyes, as if,
she feels, they are the only two on the square.

Did the remaining floor boards of vanity
begin to loosen then; did the final flush
of attendant guilt heat her cheeks?
If so, later, it had to gnaw at her
like a bad animal, his look:
grief's dark room, its one chair;
and how heavy her make-up must've felt
just then, how loud her skirts.

A confessional priest later, probably bored by lists,
piety he could not inspire,
cut off another burdened housewife:
"Be content with obeying your husband."
But she, carrying the weight heavenly voices bring,
sought another.

Domenico, meanwhile, waited impatiently for Sundays,
when he could stretch his strong legs,
lose each accomplished line on his face.
They'd walk the Corso, enjoy the great
and actual snorting of horses, which brought
undiluted nature to that dreary pock of city stone.

He loved the carriages heaped with flowers:
bowers of irises, gladiolas, would, along with his wife,

bury his face in the petals,
the shared laughter that would follow.

Anna by this time, though, could not hide
all she lacked behind pomegranate flowers
tucked against her ear, behind shows given or taken in.
She could not hide the mirrored self
she could not see, too well.

"I see you are coming against your will."

Did she feel the hypocrite as she walked,
because documents tell us she, again,
took the narrow way: another confessional door.
"Go away," the priest told her.
"You do not belong to this parish."

Without direction, she must've agonized
under insinuation:
"Who do you think you are? A nun?
No. You are not even a good wife,
playing the high and holy one,
gouging him with his need for recreation.
Well, you *were* in a hurry to marry,
weren't you, anchorite?
And so was he, if the truth be known.
You were his choice as well.
So good, now he knows what he's gotten.
Let him pay what all husbands pay,
or, better, wake up, leave him.
It's not going to work. It never does,
whatever the puppet show.
And you'll save yourself from getting clipped

when the drinking comes.... And it will come."
She went to St. Marcellus,
where their two names had become one,
risked another: sacrament.
But this time it was Father Angelo
who pulled back her veil.
"So, you have come at last!"

There are seven thousand two hundred pages in the process.
We learn that she took the barbs of discipline
as close as she could to her beating heart,
that she'd bang her Italian head on the floor
until blood gave her some hope,
perhaps, that her skull might be penetrated,
that the last vestiges of self might die,
while she still breathed and could be of use.

Consolation

By the end of 1790, they had both turned twenty-one,
Napoleon and Anna; he, soon to hold Toulon, Italy,
Corsica, Egypt; she, pregnant, a more lasting globe.
Called empty, she rounded in God's will,
even to the point of wearing a habit,
at a priest's request, in the street.

Domenico, though, put his foot down.

And Jesus agreed: "I Myself shall be your guide...
as I have always been. You question that....
Tell Me, where do you find yourself?
Beside large waters, a bee,
knee-deep in the buttercups of praise?
Isn't it tenderness you feel, each leaf moving
and yet in joyful communion?
And compunction. Doesn't your heart
long to be filled with the song that elemented it?
Isn't it humility you value now,
that bass-deep music that rejoices
in its place among the petals?

"She who wishes to hear Me
must be deaf to everything that led her here,
expect to be upbraided in turn
by each impurity which must have its say.
I make my abode in the lowly, the uncultured, the poor.
The wise and learned professors' heads
are full of the fumes of noise, prideful engines.
Live beneath them
in the stone house of contempt,
the true foundation of virtue....

"Men are like squeaking weathercocks
that spin on housetops.
If my hand did not preserve them
they would creak with every change of wind.

Roll the world, stage and gift, underfoot."

Jealous housewives helped:
"How regal she walks.
You'd think it was performance."

(These comments would become food.)

"Be wise and prudent, say, 'They mark me.'
What is it you wish, to wear an inverted crown,
or to arch under triumph, glory like a goose
in a future of stiffly passing feet?"

Signs and Wonders

And by 1790, it had begun: she saw a sun
in front of her, a globe, could range through time.
Like some Christian Teiresias, she could foresee,
hold back the heavy hand of God,
losing her human scales so that ours
might be seen, tipped.

For forty-seven years she saw the houses
and traffic of the dead:
someone humming to a ballgame,
TVs, bombers, three days of darkness;
she could hear the thoughts of people nearby or far off,
in the tone of their voices, the cut of their eye.
She could see the past, the future,
both present in the still eye of eternity.
She had only to think a thing and the Spirit
which moved her brought it to pass.
She'd walk into distant rooms
as if munching an apple,
as if she were there to inspect the curtains:
Ribwell's council chambers, a pope's jail.
She heard all the noise, and with Jesus,
bore the sin as various sects plotted
with ponderous symbol: the compass and degrees.

She would relay what she knew to the remaining cardinals;
saw ships stove, offered herself for drowning souls—
inside prisons: China, Arabia,
where confessors wasted, and still do,
under governed smiles.
She sweated blood for mission grounds,
while at twenty-one, cleaning diapers, serving her husband.

Jesus gave her the vicar's hands:
"It is I who will guide you, as the Lamb is led
by the Shepherd, as the Skull peoples all flesh."

    And finally, a peasant, someone with a wife, kids.
    I want him doing dishes quietly by an opened window
    as the days, which he knows
    have always had their own lives, march past,
    taking his. I want him to be a writer of poems,
    a pray-er. I want him to have said enough
    to one day, perhaps, collect a real pension;
    but I want him to ask himself, too,
    as we all must, have I lived?
    Have I laid enough on the line,
    have I held the soup spoon well enough?
    Will I have that honor before I find
    what will find me,
    peeled of all natural graces?

    Blessed Anna-Maria Taigi,
    I want him to say, pray for us.

THE APPRENTICE POEMS

Becoming Apprentice

Like hawks, outside of time,
perched on the limbs of winter,
the apprentice walks past
tucked Victorian houses.
Across the street a little boy shovels,
away from his dad;
he can't lift what he has gathered,
falls to his knees.
His father doesn't notice.
Perhaps he, too, feels it, the night:
rows of sprigs, pin feathers,
sprouting neatly up his back.

He'll want to move away
from the warmth,
become apprentice to cold space,
distant planets,
to Rilke's laundry woman.

He'll want to hunch out at night,
under the cover of snowy fields,
penknife in hand—;
he'll want to have it out with badgers.
He'll want to rip rural mail boxes
from their stems at night,
line them up in front of his cold,
broken hearth. Windows open,
he'll hang a large bell around his neck,
wait for his ancestors.

Come Winter

with your furtive cheeks;
write in contentious branches,
the never-stilled lake.

Beneath old ones,
tributaries of bark,
the apprentice leaps
from rock to rock,
heaves huge stones in the water,
listens to the great dunking,
walks home.

Come, Lord of purest grotesquery:
two boot dances in high snow,
the bellow which dies
before it crosses an open field.

Oh, he knows: the clouds will answer
as they always have,
raking the earth with their iron bars,
their tiny voices.

But who has time for them?

The apprentice chooses
the counter-cultural:
complete futility—Cheetoes, hooded,
in front of his cold TV,
Green Acres or the cracking of pads,
high school football.

Christmas with Ed and the Remote Control

It's dark now, and the apartment below,
vacant. His only furniture: a TV—
every local high school choir,
"A Child's Christmas in Wales,"
three Scrooge and Marley's,
a flock of *It's a Wonderful Lifes* and
Miracle on 34th Streets,
both in faded color and black and white,
Pavarotti, in costume,
and then, on another channel, in tux,
Loretta Swit in Germany,
and Florida versus UCLA—off.

The apprentice is, at last, alone,
outside—with a solitude to match the season,
Ed's bark in the distance.
The apprentice claps his deerskin mitts,
listens to the echo as his breath climbs
the ladders of Jacob
above crunching snow, the cold,
old friend, stings his thighs—
nothing but sharp, pilgrim stars
to steer the weather by.

His nose is the next to burn.
There is no escape.
He must return to his small rooms;
paint a number on each blank white wall,
so he can live where he is.

This is no life for the weary.

From his cot room he hears a clock ticking,
hears himself age in the dark:
alert to nothing, like a ball of snakes, he sits
in the ugly Christian wait.

The Apprentice, Amazed
(Christmas Time)

Oh, for the holiness which eyes the needle,
all the space it leaves in a wine glass!

Everywhere in my life, people are leaving!
Everywhere except in the crowded department stores
downtown, years ago, where chandeliers glistened
like fins of light against the ceiling—
all that holiday cheer, grunting below.

Inside his small fridge—this is what there is:
salami, a cold orange with its incredible juices.

Who would have thought life
was going to contain that!

The apprentice uses lipstick
to draw all over his face.

The Apprentice Rejoices

Verily, spring hath come,
and there is goodness in the land.
Everywhere snows recede,
everywhere, the sound of running water.

Our little sisters, the plants,
bustle over unmade beds, morning.
Mice stretch in the fields.
(Their little couches are dusty
from the long winter.)

People start going to church,
everybody walking over the earth
as if it were made of rice paper.

Everybody is Japanese this morning!
Everybody, bowing
with so much deference—
trying to make what lasts
last.

The Apprentice Wavers

What about the little tubers
that hide inside the earth?
What about them?
Do you think they go on eating
as if nothing has happened?
Some kind of cow in the brown earth?

Look! They are as abuzz as the cold water
dripping from the roof,
as an algebra book on the road.

Every earthly thing shared your joy
when you got new tires on your car.
And why not? The planet is more than dirt.

It's true. Everything has already happened!
All you have to do is be still.
Put some clothes on, wait to fill them.

Monsieur L'Amour,
send yourself some flowers,
then camp out on your front steps
with your black and white TV, beach umbrella,
lemonade. Your life will visit you
on Thursday, even before your trip
to the corner store,
with its colorful packaging, exotic peoples.

The Apprentice as Columbo

These yellow roses
which trundle in breezes
next to the rented house
are wearing overcoats!
They look like Columbo, musing,
waving their arms.

I stand in front of them,
do the same.
But it's no use,
it would never work out.

Down the street a squirrel,
is ripping up someone's tree lawn.
I'm grateful for the chaos.
It restoreth my soul,
leadeth me to still waters.

After all, nothing is as it seems.
The lawns' ways are not the squirrel's,
and the whole damned thing
rides on the night.

The Apprentice Eats Glass

Your friend, The End, comes every day:
doorbells and flowers.
He eats your grass, spackles your chimney.
Let him. He is your guest.

Invite him to sit on the porch
to share your melon, spit the seeds.
Barefoot, the two of you
can become halls of angry voices.

Hold your own,
tell him the red razor
scratches you where you itch.

He might try his long face,
tell you the radical laws of departure
are everywhere in evidence,
everywhere a bus stops
on the corner of Hollywood and time.

Join in the fun.
Tell him that half the passengers there
are dead, but to ignore them;
there is little that they can say.

The Apprentice Sees Himself in the Sunset

The lepers grew excited
beneath his window this morning,
danced like Carmen Miranda,
or a band at the Holiday Inn.

Almost immediately, he had a vision
on Third Street, a pièta:
Mother Teresa holding Jimmy Swaggart.
Some kids, off to the left, laughing,
and he hears the sound of a basketball
settling, for a second, in the chain net,
while the sky seems
like some fragile instrument
made entirely of glass.

The apprentice wants to start over,
but before he can, flowers
spring up everywhere,
like earnest Broadway farm girls.
Arm in arm, they sing "Kumbaya,"
want to buy the world a Coke.

But what would he do to live there?

He could grow out all his hairs,
work on his cross-over,
stick needles in his neck
like Alan Iverson.

Breasts start out high,
end up low.

Why be surprised at this?
It happens to everybody.

The apprentice thinks
it's this business of dying:
the cough that won't go away.
He could turn his head,
get checked for prostate cancer.

There's no privacy where he's going.

Lobster Exit

It probably *is* enough
to say one's sorry,
to regret our claws,
hold them in shame
behind our backs; to feel,
as the front of our chair is removed,
the depths of our plated natures;
to feel the grace, the mud we flop in,
to warm to garbage.
It's probably enough to feel
the cold blood pulse at our throats,
to crawl self-consciously
across the floor with that slight
side-to-side motion,
to hear the tac-tac sounds
our claws make on the tiles
as people, embarrassed, move chairs
to make way.
It's probably good to see
an antenna occasionally bob before us
as we try to hold up a good front,
march boldly through our secretions
toward the door.

The Apprentice Considers Fleas

The flea on your bed at night
has such tiny feet!
He treks in moonlight
across white dunes.
The buzz of his feelers
occupies all of his attention.
He seldom gives a thought
for his brother who is in Timbuktu
or for the rice on the kitchen floor.

And the moon! It is there
and bathes him in such light!
He could almost stop,
grab a cigarette. But does he?
No, I tell you. He marches on,
little soldier, the Duke, his will,
hard as an abandoned button,
his joy, as real
as the Ayatollah's honeymoon.

This world depends on him.
He knows this.
He has to be where he is:
his step into
his step.

Siphonaptera,
he has a barbed mouth,
speaks many languages,
but who could listen to him
tear himself?

There is no loneliness like his!
Not in all the world!

The Apprentice Sings A Cappella

If you want the truth
you must look for it.
It's that simple.
If it's there, it will stick a foot out
as you pass.
He will hold his side
laughing as you fall,
like an insurance salesman
from Nebraska.

It will be more than you expected.

But then, of course,
you must decide
what you're going to do with him.
He might follow you into the Deli,
maybe say something about the Jews.
You can just picture him
down on the corner with the boys,
trying to fit in over the evening fire,
with his wide-open polyester suit,
his white belt.

(Your friends will hate him,
but won't be able to ask him to leave
because of his size.)

He'll try to sing the bass part,
completely destroy the harmony.

No sir,
you won't be able to take him anywhere.

The Apprentice Prophesies

You'll be amazed by flat-black steel porch rail
in sunlight, the black mailbox behind that: the brick,
texture and grain.
You'll be struck dumb by the ordinary,
and everything will start to matter:
what shirt you put on,
how to pronounce your name.

You'll start helping dogs across the street,
being careful not to cycle over worms after rain.
You and the whole neighborhood,
everyone with quick, uncertain wheels,
hand brakes and balance.
You'll come home hours later,
muddy, but happy.

You'll keep waiting for it to end.

The Apprentice Considers His Addiction

The Apprentice is as slick as Vermont maple.
After a shower he greases his hair back,
checks his aquiline nose.

He makes cameo appearances at 7-11s,
eats little powdered donuts
in the back of the store,
gets the white stuff of wisdom
on his beard.

He is your brother, mother;
He is the socks in your drawer:
a sprawl of ganglia, nerve-endings,
and he will go out with your daughter.

And so, if on the street,
he offers you one of his marshmallows,
eat quickly through the pale skin,
catch the gooey center
where the mercury is pure.
There you will find all the cars,
all the traffic in the world.

Give him your granules, not your love,
a pound of confectioners.

He will move faster
than the recovering economy,
buying and selling, faster and faster:
lamps, watches, dental floss, condos,
whole agencies, fast enough to keep his place

in this world,
this world in its rightful place.

The Apprentice's New Job
(Lunch hour)

The apprentice thanks God
for his little friends, neuroses.
They keep him in line.

"Be glad and clap your hands
when you are alone," he tells himself.
"When else is it so clear
that you are not?"

He munches bananas
on the top of cliffside rocks,
flings his peels to the trees below,
branches sagging
like business opportunities.

The sky is so bright today,
it leaves teeth marks on his soul.

"More light," a dying Goethe said,
"I can still see."

The Apprentice and the Egg

Consider them,
so round and romantic,
perfect in every way.
They are what they are,
not some abstract,
oblong syllables of death.

No. They have taken up residence here—
in our houses, delighting in the space they use,
in their almost unobtrusive lifestyles.
(You can tell that by the way they stand
in the carton, the arabesque figure
each one cuts,
their almost military reserve.)

They stand against us.
(We are not their measurers!
We may not have their pasts!)

So how shall the apprentice live then?

Sam Cooke will teach him
the cha-cha-cha.
He will go on tour: Seattle, Ashtabula,
do regional TV coffee clatches,
meet and discuss deep topics
with many women anchors.

He will learn how to give
successful halftime motivational speeches,

will make brief stops at 1600 PA Ave.,
the new cabinet member:
Minister of the Paleolithic,
chorus of the night.

SOME KIND OF PILGRIM

Ten-hour Layover: Greyhound Station
(Davenport, IA)

Bound for a life of pool hall hyperbole,
an overweight kid talks too loud, all the time:
to the station master, to anyone who will listen.
The high hitch in his pants has given him acne,
and sitting next to a Brylcreamed Polonius;
they both watch
as the wise man's cigarette, slowly,
right in front of them, becomes symbol—
Dean Moriarity!

(During my wait, I see him get hired and fired
as help around the station.)

Two teenage girls hang as well, popping gums,
rolls of flesh arguing tight shirts.
One asks me, "Mister," for a quarter,
later offers Burger King coupons.
Like her speeding boyfriend who is wired up and thin, pasty,
she's down for a night of urban stairwells, cheap wine.

My bus finally comes—
but they never take me far,
no matter where I'm going. Like the rest here,
I ride them because there's no place for me yet in America.
It hasn't been invented.
Call the coach "idling pumpkin"
or "mobile project housing":
a ghetto for waifs, not-evers, anti-presidents;
one more poor place nobody visits,
which is too bad,
because where else are things so real?

Winter

The frozen blue salt
crunches on the platform
after another long day of banging jaws:
the strap of a freight elevator,
of packing display signs into thin boxes,
fingerprints worn raw
at handling of cold cardboard.
Just three of us and aisles
of pallets, neatly stacked
in a cavernous warehouse.

Cars underneath the overpass
seem to hunker down in the bitter cold,
in the slow, sure grind of frozen rubber,
inching over treads of snow.
They seem to weigh each movement—
energy expended.
Through wisps of monoxide,
they speak grudgingly,
and even then, only when spoken to;
the nearly steel, concrete,
each bitter as breakdown.

Eels of snow rattle,
test the chain link fence
along one side of the road,
burn our faces, exposed wrists,
each person, tramping for all he's worth
on the platform, huddling in his coat
until, finally, the rails ring: broken, cold,
as approaching Rapid Transit lights
in the dusk search them out,

spent variations, individualized
under years of existential weight, speed,
in this snow which flurries before the train
with its welcome, if artificial heat

inside:
passengers, gloriously new,
each so given over to the new climate
for the first minute or two of confinement
that those who choose to sit in aisle seats
don't even bother to unbutton,
choose rather, to stretch their cold legs,
then rub them until the stinging cold joy
begins, almost regretfully,
to subside.

A Tribute to Old Municipal Stadium
(late '80s: playoffs vs. the Colts)

Conjuring winter, we pay for the elephant dance:
ripped up sod on the stadium floor,
the rumbling roar which is the cold backs of bears
or shelves of shale along the Cuyahoga,
rising: Cleveland and the Browns.

The small trees outside stand at attention.
Their spines begin to prickle,
having been gnawed on by the ravenous larvae
of prehistoric birds.

Inside, I play Aaron, hold up my cousin's arms
until we score. It is the stadium that does this,
so old that it is a monument to death,
with its slatted seats, the gray lake outside,
pounding; nature's ice sculptures:
the vertical thrust and radically frozen curves
I once saw on TV during a different game,
lake water frozen above a concrete wall,
a man fishing in the nook below.

It's third and ten: beers on a bitterly cold day,
a half-empty flask of Jack under my sock.

Bring on your foreign teams, Mr. Death.
We live here.

Cleveland, December

Driving down Green Rd., across from the warehouse
for the mentally retarded where I used to work,
the field spreads out in tall, wet, weighted orange grass,
the occasional arms-and-elbows adolescent tree.
In the distance, a core of bristle, an earthen comb: trees
along the horizon—seepage, and closer,
a ticking among branches. Gray clouds,
like a rush of gray hands, beat seasonal drums.

It would've been nice to have pulled over,
opened the door of my '69 Tempest,
stray molding flapping against brackets,
and, squishing in the mud,
a cabin built there.

But this is not Innisfree.
(And they don't have cable.)
Besides, all our bees caught a mite last summer
and are dead. Nothing worth keeping
allows you to, even people,
spilling ridiculously into one another
on the sub-atomic level
as we talk, almost solids: our skin, membrane,
a relaxed weave.

Like sheriff Ez, nothing coheres.

Nope. God has no dignity.
Think of those tiny cameras inside the human heart,
catching the valves in action.
What kind of machines are those lops of skin,

responding like little soldiers to impulses,
not a classical line or angle anywhere?

Everything is beyond us: the stars, our hands,
any point spread you can name.
How did we get here? And where are we going?
We live in such mystery it makes me wonder
who invented red-tag sales?
And why don't I *feel* like this is my body?

Case #29061: Memphis Slim

Glenn, a tall and skinny black teen,
is heading for the University of LaSalle,
wants to run in the next Olympics:
an "out-of-state track champ."
When he comes back from his guided evening runs,
he holds his face closer to yours
than you'd like, so you can see the sweat,
that barely traceable edge of violence,
which is real; and so, for longer than you'd like,
you watch him,
man your precipice.

Mr. Death

I, too, get to go through it—
like all those before me: Moses,
Eleanor of Aquitaine, Little Sister Amen,
every duck, ostrich.

Will there be paintings on those walls,
a "St. Francis slept here"?
I think there'll be an old couch or two,
Tommy Dorsey records.
The carpet won't be much,
but I'm going barefoot.

I'll bring what I can of my friends, my wife, my children;
I'll crowd memories like sparrows around me—

The sigh you won't hear will be my last goodbye:
my hand and the clear knob
I won't want to turn.

California, Dreaming

Up from a gull airfield, dwarfed by sand,
Long Beach stone, I thought of Goleta:
low-tide winter beach, wet-suited surfers,
the last sorry waves in the twilight.
How we'd be up early, power chunks of hash.
Then b-ball. Craig and Gary, a native,
made screws for a living,
vying for the best one each day.
They lived a kind of manufactured madness,
longed for the wry hipness, holiness
which might transform them,
settled for a kind of show.
I left them their generosity,
went south, to the LA basin,
Queen Mary, California, a place
no more my own than home,
than the people there I never spoke to,
than what moved me through those places.

Sitting above smashing foam, rock,
I thought of the tattooed people, beach front parlors,
those who'd made their marks—external.
They were blunt enough
to know what they lacked: beauty
badges, flexing in the oddness that binds us all,
too far from home.

And then, much later,
I heard that Craig had killed himself,
having driven his car off a cliff
to spite some sunny California girl,
making wry commentary as he did.

California was always like that for me:
other.

Once I abbey-sat for monks in Redwood Valley,
and when they got back from the Holy Land,
Father Michael offered me some chocolates,
cleaning off the maggots.

"Have some California," he might have said,
"But not too much."

Every place is like that, of course,
has to be, because there's no fiction
like home—. Still, I'd give a lot to be back there:
in Cleveland, near those friends who were never
as close or real as I would have liked,
near the memories we never shared,
the places that didn't exist.

Still, it would be close: Lake Erie,
vast in steel blue, gray, driving in
on the eastern shoreway, summers,
evening's huge orange sun
beginning to settle down, squeezing
between blue clouds,
and to the left, tinted skyline.

I'm a lake person, not this Ohio,
with its river hills, skinny houses.
If it were my call to make, I'd set up camp
at Mark's house, near the lake, the one he lent me
one summer to write poems in.

I'd go to Indians' games,
no matter how bad they became—
with each friend, such as he or she is.
We could talk poetry or politics,
Alberts: Belle or Luplow.

Do we ever really like the places where we live
when we're there? For a while maybe,
but then the wishing starts all over again:
for finer, bigger or older homes, hipper places.

Elizabeth Bishop was right!
We have no home here,
and there is no chance of finding one.

This is a grace.

Nursing Home, Third Shift
(after C. K. Williams)

A new guy, off a first heart attack, would try to slug me
when I changed his diaper ("Depends" they called them),
as I removed the waste, wiped the back of his balls.
And Horace, who'd cry out "Pee-pee, pee-pee" every time
I made rounds. I'd have to crouch a little bit when I'd take
him to the bathroom as he shuffled, my hands under
his elbows. (Sometimes I'd make noises like a train.)
Mornings he dressed easy, but I wondered if he'd just
be on that couch all day, waiting for meals, movement.
Charlie was ambulatory, loved the Tigers, his old Japanese
transistor radio pressed to his ear, in front of the TV,
catching the late game from the coast. He could only
mumble, but was happy. That year they won the pennant.
There was an old lady who used to talk non-stop
whenever I potted her: the town's long gone Heinz plant,
her family's history. And Joanie, too old to talk,
but with a little girl's smile. She'd been a teacher,
liked her sock dolly with her when, in the mornings,
I'd strap her into her chair. They were soft, padded,
and the early morning women workers cheerful.

But there was Mary, too, the owner's speechless mother,
who would occasionally play the coquette, imagine
she was being dressed by her livery, a man who hung
on her every strap.

I quit finally. Work hours cut in half without notice—
a fundamentalist woman resident, who'd discovered
I was Catholic, claimed I'd stolen money. (The staff
had even put a fiver out as bait for awhile, half hidden
among the meds; sent a cop over to my room.)

But I was tired, too, tired of going home, smelling of urine,
tired of a hemmed-in existence: work, another ridiculous
grad school, my tiny room next to train tracks.
Beer and crumbs of literary talk aside, it was like walking
through my own dark soul, those streets at night.
Absurd too, what with that drop-dead student strumpet
across the hall—and me, a Christian.

And then the mornings would come, and I'd put on
my composition face, not one answer felt along
the breakable bone.

And though those old folks were like most people,
living because, on some level, they liked it; and despite
the fact that it was probably good for them: babies again,
in diapers, being changed and touched a lot, people
enjoying them, not because of what they brought
to a conversation, but because they were alive—
they were no better off than I, scuffling with enfeebled
birdlike hands, trying to unearth lives
which are never forthcoming.

Marian Sector II

Wet boots, a slightly packed snow field,
trees glazed, under a gray sky;
streaks, finger-painted clouds,
ground to woodchuck ground.

Flakes begin to fall, thick now,
as a Rambler over deep snow.
The young trees are bare, sticks, or your life.
You touch them, with sweaty hands,
having taken off your layered mitts:
the deerskin, the wool.
The bark is rough, slick,
seems to cut at your fingers.

You pass.

In the morning,
when the sun has taken its fill from tall crystal,
flowers, from gutters, and rises, half drunk,
like a cowboy in the Hand which holds it,
and you find yourself alone, again, at breakfast,
face deep in pollen, drowning: alive
as the white sword is drawn
from its pink sheath, your heart.

She is there, with you, looking out
past the curtains
to the stars, the roundness of the sea.

To possess nothing, all of it.
This is your end.
To feel yourself rise in conversation,
ignore it, go on talking.
To become so small
that there is finally room for you
on the sidewalk.

The plain wooden statue,
and on the way up to Communion,
on the left cheek, a tear glistening.

She is a door that signals procession,
the kind you feel, sometimes, mornings,
stopping your bicycle in a graveyard,
each person, one day, rising, walking east
through cold grass, dissipating mist.

You will be among them.

Beaded tears on grotto floors.

We recite them, drone, as if at a funeral,
count our sins, the days we left
on the road to Sodom,
the days of wheat and barley,
of fast talking, back slapping.

They are our cry,
they are her answer.

We do not know what is to come. We know
what is here.

Out There
(ten of us)

We were the Catholic menace in gray shingle,
farmhouse to their almost suburban tracts.
My parents must've seemed communist in kids,
our house facing the main road,
backyard, more dirt than grass,
opened to their edged side street.
My brothers, to the chagrin of neighbors,
built a fort in the oldest tree thereabouts,
in our backyard, would push kids out of it,
flip darts at their calves as they ran away.
Protestant mothers were horrified,
kept juniors, in Bermudas, at bay.

But we had the only apple tree,
and those rebellious Protestants
could climb as high as any of us,
to the crack of branches, splitting bark:
the fibrous wood flower splintering,
as we fished far out for the best green globes.
The clouds were up there, the sun,
and all of us, on bikes after,
to Gunnings for a swim.

Sure, my brothers were crazed: Tim chasing Pat
with an ax, minor police investigations.
And my father, limping some on his high
polio shoe, '55 Ford–red wagon in the street,
dressed like the embarrassingly
blue-collar worker he was.

Once or twice he played with us out back,
tried to teach an, even by then,
old-time from-the-chest bounce pass,
to the extent that we'd let him—
because we were angry at him too,
hated him some, for how often
he'd not done as much.

But he deserved better from us, from me,
was one of the first WWII soldiers
to get Survivor's Leave, having spent eight hours
in shark-infested Guadalcanal waters,
water which, years later, he told me
from a psych ward hospital bed,
had broken him.

It's too late, I know, but I want to thank him
for his one skinny polio arm,
the flapping underneath part, which moved
counter-point to his body as he played with us.
It took courage to show that,
I knew even then, in those late Eisenhower,
early Kennedy years—to so publicly reveal a deformity;
and I'm glad, too, that part of him
was telling that whole uptight "blessed"
perseverance-of-the-saints neighborhood
that they could kiss his ass
if they didn't like his life.

Late, in Battle
(after C. K. Williams)

In a cramped VA hospital room with Mom, Dick,
a miniature TV on a portable arm, you shuffled papers,
phone pressed between neck and ear;
and though I didn't recognize it then, I can see now
you were putting yours in order.

It was a constant pain, your back. You were looking
at a wheelchair life when Dick found you, the wrong
night time pills out of so many. It was not
that you lacked will. Two days after your last operation,
staples intact, you walked the five miles home at night
cursing doctors.

But I never saw that other side: the dark knowledge,
surety that your time was almost up—that the game
had been played out: Nam copters, landing on your back,
shrapnel, too many jobs, wives.

But do we all get what you had that day, I want to know:
the grace, the wrap in our suffering; do we all
get to style a little bit before we go? Tim, we're all
soldiers here, tramping through our lives, wrestling badly
with what binds up, taking no prisoners because none
will have us.

Look in on us once in a while. There will be nights
when I'll be up, the moon high above our dark, wet street.
Look in on your nephew and godson,
who is learning to live here. Teach him: the beauty

and value of the physical world, yes; but of what will
take us, too, blind as moles, shuck us—down,
as we begin to suffocate, flail in the darkness,
wait for the Mercy which waits
just beyond our reach.

A Poem Delivered
(for my sister and her son)

Twenty years old, the family torch-bearer—
into the grave. Those eyes, half open
on the coroner's table, reminding her
of his own when he slept as a baby.

The pride of her motherly life,
murdered, deftly stabbed beneath his arm,
dying face down in a parking lot after beers,
and then the assailant,
reading his Bible in court,
turning toward her, again, to grin.

He got off, and Chuck can't even work,
though Larry wasn't his biological son;
he rages at younger brother Patrick,
who is only in jail.

It took us all: Larry, the solid, the jock,
with his girl Carmen, an unfortunate time
in the Navy behind him, his expression so even
that it would never give more away
than what he would ask for himself.

I wonder what kind of sisterly strength
can bear this, not to mention her youngest,
a girl, also in jail, and the oldest, in Denver,
who calls a wealthy Evangelical "Mom."

My life's been easy.
I, who have always thought of myself
as strong, have been pampered, kept safe,
apart, a dull Thérèse, while she,
who had only sought to drift
beneath the currents of the times,
survives like Stonehenge.

I missed him once strike out seventeen kids
in a six-inning little league game,
the last few years of his life, really;
his time flying by me, like my own,
and what, what can I claim at this moment?
This "here," this "now," where no one else lives,
where any other person is just guest,
even my wife who has given me such children?

They are the altars we build for the Most High,
in the hopes that He will take them, and us
when the time comes,
which will always be too soon:
our lives, as Mary has said,
a wave of a hand.

What They Gave
(for Larry, my brother)

1.

I wanted to talk: your girl, Linda,
blown away—stepfather's impotent rage,
him falling drunk, all over her words, his gun.

And then she's dead.
And the old man?
He probably fell, passed out,
wetting himself under all those fierce stars.

We sat in high weeds, next to the garage, streetlight.
Tears you had rubbed away flattened blond hairs
high on the walls of your cheek.

Physical affection did not run in our family.
Our parents loved us,
but had to watch from a distance
as the dust of all those summer days, the tears,
gave us a skin.

This is what they gave.

2.

Remember Grandma Spilker's voice,
always so high, urgent,
because life, even before her young husband's death,
the Depression, must've flattened her early;
her gray hair, looking like a light socket
had gotten the best of her;
that white gouge in her cheek!

I was with her just before she died:
spots of white, a black and red cancer
curling what was left of her tongue.
Terrified, she could no longer talk,
but screamed without restraint.

And when I asked her to wait,
told her that Jesus would come,
she shot me such a suspicious look
that I cowed, felt a fraud, despite my faith.

But I said it again—
what I had never seen.

The nuns said she died in peace shortly after.
But did you know that I'd prayed for that very experience
six months before at the Christian Life Center:
someone witnessing
about helping another to heaven?

There is so much pain in this life, Larry,
(other friends dying senselessly, too, later)
so much of it in our own hearts, family,
that you'd never think things so twisted
could be set right.

But the years have marked us, brother,
each time chaos has reared its many heads.

Maybe they didn't do such a bad job.

Parked Taxi
(Ft. Collins, CO)

Sitting through a skiff of wind,
my ship skidding sideways into port,
long dead leaves over the curb, the tide.

"Board's clear."

A dark argument goes on in the tops of six a.m. trees,
a determined tossing; and on the FM, as if to answer,
violins and orchestra!   .

I wait, play this oaten flute for the crows in the field,
for the gray and seedless days
which number twenty-five in my opened palm.

There is no way out;
like the leaves, I will die to what I know of myself,
if my attachments precede me or not.
I'll get caught in some similar breeze,
under the same gray-bellied clouds.

So let me play like David on his harp,
joyfully, ignorant of everything beyond the now,
or the Company Who is too quiet
for these words.

Curling in the Checker seat,
a pad on my lap, I make like Li Po,
toss in the cursive stems of these upheavals,
mountain flowers.

Christmas Night Cab Stand
(Ft. Collins, CO)

Jupiter, in the early evening,
shines like Bethlehem over the crescent;
pale blue, the moon's northeastern side.
And earlier, the mist in front of the foothills,
the foothills themselves,
both colored slate as the last light
worked its way down through clouds, the peaks.
Scraggy cottonwoods, distant,
muted in what light there was,
could have been palms!

Nearer, condos, like generous hands,
seemed to rise up, offer themselves
out of the soft brown earth.

33rd Birthday Poem

I.

On a sailboat blue, clear Colorado
winter afternoon, wind and the brisk
flapping of pantleg!
The sky could've been great petals curling!

Near the highway, above tall grass,
roadside concrete duct,
a muskrat dove into home waters;
then a tree's bark, on my way to the town library,
seemed to mass like sinew:
the power that moves all creation!

I saw it earlier too, that morning,
parked out on the high plains,
a mile or so in front of distant trees,
which seemed to perch
like irregular prehistoric stones
against the pre-dawn sky: the orange
gathering, slowly eclipsing
the russet, the pinks;

and then the steering wheel,
the backs of my hands...

2.

My 33rd, and tonight, one of my fares
walked up to a guy on his doorstep, decked him.
He then turned crisply, walked back to the cab:
something about (the politics of) five grand.

The ignorance he insisted I offer the police
was not a stretch
since it wraps me in this night, under pale stars,
the faint stirrings of mushrooms,
their final heads
breaking through soft crusts of soil.

"This is my body," the ground says,
and for that moment, everything that listens
can finally be heard.

The Edges of Mercy

Colorado blue, small city taxi days:
glacial flows on the north sides of houses,
streets, snow-filled early,
wet and steaming in the afternoon sun;
this guy I was taking to the VA in Cheyenne,
all over the back seat mirror,
talking to himself, to me:
"So are you going to turn me in,
or *what?*"

(Days later he stabbed someone in a Boulder bar.)

Another guy, still in Nam, wore a neck brace,
was, like his woman who never disguised
her hatred of him, as blond and tan
as he wanted to be.
He *knew* how much his voice grated,
that was the thing that got me:
the fraying twine of it when we were alone,
pieces of his cracked will
all over the back seat. And he wouldn't let up.
He'd talk, just so I could hear the bodies of the dead
bob up, bloat in the Mekong Delta.
I felt like Sartre in hell, the meter exacting
just how much time I had to pay
as I drove him to liquor stores, Denny's,
to late night construction sites:
looking for parties which never materialized.

There was this Chicano, too, who'd be lit every morning,
going to or coming from the bar, his mother's house.
He'd dig out his belches with a ritualized hand,
fisting at the waist.
"I was born naked," he'd say.
"Now I've got a pair of pants.
To hell with the parade."

But I could write poems, too,
cruise down wide streets, grassy divides,
feel like Rockefeller in my old clothes.
I could ride the Overland Trail next to mountains,
pick up some guy out there
who'd be cursing, screen door and his woman,
banging behind him, a couple of Colorado chickens
squawking in his wake.

None of it ever got any of us home, of course,
each of us wanting our lives so badly
that they fed on everything else,
the stuff of repentance, praise finally,
if you choose to see it that way:
a hundred reasons daily to pick your feet up,
a hundred reasons to put them down again—
wearing out the soles of your traveling shoes.

Possum

White-faced, spare fur, he stood hunched, slowed,
in the middle of the country road.
He bobbed, almost imperceptibly,
lifting his front paws, mouth,
blood and spittle along a teeth line
he could not, with gravity, altogether close.
I saw him struggle, dying in the worst, the only
possible way: silently, alone.

I watched for awhile, got out of the car,
sat down as near to him as I could.

Death, here is thy sting:
you sit there, at the end of our lives,
like some huge oblivious bear,
close enough to us to be a threat,
but unconcerned, your chin lolling along your fat chest,
up and down, caught in the flies above your head,
your own preserve.

It's too much.

I want to ask, "Why don't we cut cards or something?"
But you are a bear and won't talk.
A whiff of honey, a sun bright enough to make you squint;
that's as far as you go.

Possums and people die,
each on his own stage.
And a person, if he is blessed, might get to see it beforehand,
the walnut hard casing of his life,
the packed dirt he grows between
in this vast and glorious vegetable kingdom.

Assumption
(Copper Country, U.P.)

1.

Up in Finnish Ahmeek, in a county
where there were more bears and pasties than people,
Barb and John were their usual what-ho selves,
full of regional talk, poetic amazement.

The country up there was so unspoiled:
Sioux St. Marie and cabin rentals for six bucks
along the inner shore, hitching in.

2.

Outside their chalked Franciscan church window,
fields foamed yellow in flowers;
the river, rattling like children
over gaunt gray shoes: stones;
while clouds, like Superior frigates, steamed past.

Inside, up front, Barb's son, Ian, held the paten.
His eyes were a cold blue, and, at ten,
they ran like northern waters, following each creak in the pews
as if he had talons.

I went up with John, Barbara holding the chalice.
A whole line of us went up:
all the church workers, Stroh burners.
That over-bearing blue-bellied captain of the bazaar tent team
went up, too, minus the swagger and boom;
went up with his wife and retarded daughter,
who was bigger than I: childlike, clean, shaven.

As usual, I had the guy wrong.
His burden was right out there for everyone to see;
every Sunday during communion, every other day too,
carrying his daughter.

Thrown head-first into courage,
pushed that way, he was given the girl
because he could bear it, loudly,
for the rest of us, because God was listening.

3.
I keep trying to get my way back up there,
to that country, with my own family now,
an eight-year old Down's child of my own.

Barb's remarried again, to a Finn this time.
I would like to see her fresh, older face now,
the cane she uses to get herself around.

The water was so clean;
people with cabins could run underground hoses
way out into the biggest lake on the continent,
drink that. Then.
Even the woods seemed new.

But that's how it goes around here
in the Catholic capitol of Steubenville:
even local acquaintances lapse so long
that their kids look huge the next time you see them,

all the while your own troupe tests you and every day they see—
and this new puppy we just got,
a Miniature Schnauzer named, what else, Harry Potter,
he races around on back yard command,
face skidding so low in the turns that his snout gets caught
in the sod, flips him over.
But the thing is, that doesn't stop him.
He just goes all out again after that, running
just to run, as if he knows better than any of us
that there's no such thing as tomorrow.

Two Gratitudes
> Praise
> and narrow is the way

My Own rejoiced in a Kansas barn,
second story dust, in the sledge hammer,
the shredding planks, spreading sunlight.

With His eyes, halfway up,
I could enjoy the wheat, the trees, the sky;
that old beat pick-up
coming small, up the road.

(Blisters had finally stopped me short—
and I knew the game was over.
With wet, stinging hands, I had to sit, wait.
There would be no job there, no beautiful Prairie Paula,
my having hitched out;
no life quite so replete with symbol.)

Young and invincible,
what was one more absurd stop
on the Jesus-and-His-Church road to heaven?

Youth spreads it arms out wide,
praises God for all that it sees.
That is what it does the best.

Age does so too, having, thankfully,
acquired a wryer gratitude.

On Grace

My wife puts on the cellulite video,
gets caught throughout, between commands,
trying to get the last one right before this one's done.
She has enthusiasm, does the grapevine,
arms swinging up too late, and then back, behind her,
The clap.

I think of her high school cheerleading try-outs,
how the panel of student judges
called her out a second time, just to laugh.

But she was there, doing the routine again:
the jumps, the yells, willing to try
because that is all we get, the now, the mistakes
that sometimes lapse too close to perfection.
Pushing her glasses up her nose, she looks at me,
smiles: these birth pounds have to come off.
And her husband, the man who's turned from his book—
needs to see.

For the Joy of It

I Saw All the Forgiven

I saw all the forgiven
in a wide opened cathedral
I saw banners waving
shouting   praising

I saw the forest darken
as we   zipped and sweaty   dirt-biked
roared flaps up through water
tailed in sand

I saw the bottle-necked sun
tincture red   set
I saw clouds turn red as I sat barefooted
on a shingled roof

Iron Fence

Twenty furred young sparrows tuck
on a cold young tree
next to the old black stone church downtown
buildings and a crunchy blue sky

People scurry   it's six degrees
a stoplight waits beyond
this cold pointed black iron fence

The Presence of God
(Downtown Steubenville)

He spoke in a thimble
a choir of pigeons   necking about
long peals   rakes of ice: railroad tracks
in front of toothless buildings   hollow
corridor smiles and the
bite in frozen grass

up they flew
and over
me and every spider wire

a cold hissing   soft
under the flap
and feather of muscled wings

Pentecost

Who is this Holy Spirit?
And what is He doing in the eggplant?

Your Feet
(for Susan)

I never knew I
carried your smile

would want to bury myself
in black wet soil

could kiss God's soft mouth
that He would kiss me back

but I always knew
I'd want to wash your wide feet

Reflection: 105 degrees
(Denver)

Yes
these rough fingers would hold the flow
of your kinked-at-the-roots island hair

I would watch you   crooked woman
like water fountaining from the hose
carry you on sun wheels up driveways
with buckets of gravel
like I do my stalk green self   shovel shine in
the friction in a half ton of that stone

Come   there are basements to rip out
chunks of concrete and singe of hot metal
forearms from the insides of dump trucks doors
there are trenches to be dug
plastic pipe and sump pumps to be sunk
there is beer after

> Tonight I look up   through the skylight
> from the kitchen table   say
> "I will sweep the corners of this great night bone,
> wipe the little windows clean"

Apple Fools
(Madonna House)

Apple fools   we are
Ripe as cups of cider and the horse's
clodded wake

Let the wet mornings come   ring out
green beans beneath the leaves   pumpkin
piping on the vine
Speckled corn aloft   Indian feathered
high on the door

Squash squats on the rafters
pot belly   bent legged   Buddha stove
boots and coveralls
Give us this grace and all this day
the crowded table
the pinion's fold.

Ash Wednesday
(Puerto Rico)

The treed hills   carpet green
cows slipped in and out of view

Under plywood roof
mismatched chairs   table and a breeze
coconut's milk   pianono
You canvassed my past   I watched you move
Children   three on a bike   sounded the asphalt
through palms and flourish of undergrowth

The ocean was green...

                        you were beautiful

We met in moccasin   season
our completion smoothed us like stone

At night the ocean rolled
without distraction
(we could have been the shore)
Sand like glass
stars and an arching moon

You wanted to make love on the beach
I said   you to me   forever

African Shoes
(Ft. Collins Yellow Cab)

There are small bone-shaped heads which come up
in the frosted grass   winter mornings
They are the size of African shoes
They are   angels

Large hands rattle the fake fronts
of western style buildings

There are angels' wings
in the mountains   They make noises
like old machinery

The metal fence post   the strung barbed wire
become illumined   cold grass burns and
the small voice
passes

Spring, to Work

There is stone in negative earth
As I wait for my bus
buildings   like hands
praise

Sap-in-the-Wood   here   in the suburbs
trees billow green smoke across
a pertinent field

Down the paved   country road
wet bark blossoms in shells and
a mandate of rock costs the stream only time
only hours

Cantaloupe flowers ride the pine
masted   in the tuck
of turtle lake

Up the walk in front of the Detention Home
In pink blossoms
white rafts
blossoms wet on the cattled ground

The Light Behind the Imagination

a yellow taxi
yellow leaves

no calls
and from the spacious front Checker seat
the wrap-around glass
a large tree ahead
Leaves gone at the top like a
woman's back   her robe
dropping from her shoulder
(or   leaves   a hive of busy
shivering bees)

off to the right
a tanned shirtless roofer unrolls tarpaper
along a low-pitched roof
The sound of his hammer
catch the glittering nails
"See this," they say.
"This is what lasts."

New York in Broad Daylight
(for Jack)

In sunny Central Park
I see Him,
a Child flying a Japanese kite,
the kite itself. Pot-bellied,
He plays a hot corner.

He waves beneath His chin,
jogs uphill with the horde, and I feel
all the grass growing inside me.
Great gray buildings
become mice. Blind, they crawl, new-born,
squeaking. Painting along the sidewalk
learn French, drink coffee.

A Julliard student plays viola
to my violin:
the careful crunch of cheesecake,
Village Café. And later,
all the small people inside me bop,
the Flintstone theme on sax, Washington Park.
I see Him, with brush and can,
face streaked,
as billowing orange letters,
noisy cars, zip past.

Young Monk
(Denver)

Wine, water,
like the red patch, yellow body of a peach
in a bowl, sit
behind layers of fine lacquer,
two millennia of pews
in the bowels of the dark Catholic Church.
And on the cross up front,
on the wall behind the gold,
the altar, I feel the Body, the wound,
in new water, draw;
feel the corresponding motion
without noise.

Mass and, after, outside,
capped clothespins hold the flapping
bedsheet canvas, day: yellow sun head
tucked in a coat of trailing
above-the-trees-wrap-around blue.
Garrulous birds and the sweet
smell of pine needle.

A calling. Fine as my stride,
elevated as the caps of waves,
spray and shingle, celibate air.

This life for Life
and a walk through the trees.

Cleveland

Rises:
the Sohio, National City, Huntington Bank:
shoulders nudging, great white galleys in
an ocean mined red in cuts and coral,
hot copper solder, long digital mornings.

In traffic, the number 6 bus,
sewer caps, the warm orange of the engines;
down 9th: river whistles, temperature readings,
a house in every passing eye, the kraut and dogs,
the commerce of bread and utensils, minus any sway
toward the slow moving rains.

On sunny days, there is a keyboard
in the independent movement
of flowers, in the bright yellow and black jacket:
vibrations, the colors of bees;
old Gaelic crosses, courtyards.
                    Listen…
on a quiet evening, you can hear it
in the knocking of moored boats all
the way to Sandusky Bay; between the cobbles
downtown, off 13th,
where aging softball players tee up,
rip golf balls off a corrugated cat-walk, a warehouse,
watch them land on the roof of the Trailways
bus terminal. It speaks in every bottle there
on the sidewalk; in Ralph,

the bartender's lisp, inside,
                    "Christ, wat asshoes,"
as he speaks to the old-timer,
the one who once asked me
up to his room, told me I could try
on some of his new clothes.

SONNETS FROM MATTHEW

God's Book Comes After His Plan
(Matthew 1: 1-17)

God's book comes after His plan. How the King of time
must shake His shaggy head and laugh as we
insist on our smaller scripts. We write the lines
for a play that no one else will ever see.
Not a jot or tittle of our presumption will reach
the light of day. Each will be burnt away
with every other falsehood we bother to teach,
every bit of wisdom we save to say.
He makes His door through the houses of the poor.
And when His mercy takes the back lots of our lives,
our petals receive. He bees a pollen store,
heaps us summer, in leaves, and our fictions thrive.
From the Self of heaven, Heaven becomes the man
who dies, so his bones can cleave, his sinews find hands.

Her Days Passed in Breezes
(Matthew 1: 18-25)

Her days passed in breezes, palm trees at noon,
the granular water jar as it scraped along
the top of the well. But this world, though fair, was a tomb
to be dusted, too, a glorious, passing wrong-
headed Eden, like the law of God which stored
its living bones, which coaxed loose tongues to flame:
"Messiah": fire-like whispers, sheath and sword—.

But *what* human heart could bear that Name?

And Joseph? He lived between Mosaic lines:
the splints of freedom. God's law was the only school
for a hasty man. In scroll or dreams, those signs
were heaven: his lot now, to pray with a carpenter's tools.

As husbands, wives do, they kept their daily pace.
Through grace and circumstance He shows His face.

Nocturn, After Auden
(Matthew 2: 1-12)

The teachers of the law, the people's priests,
sit on their parchment and sneer: "Foreigners chasing
a star!" And Herod is left, on gilded seat,
to put on civic order's tiresome face:
"Oh Bethlehem, what have you done to my profits?"
Had he winter's colder eye, its timeless expanse
inside, he might have had a love for it,
holy poverty: God's "always-with-us" dance.
And what of the kings? They were giddy, "overjoyed,"
the text relates. But did they so thirst for what
would free them that they neglected the serpent's ploys?
Did they trade their cities, learning, for berries and nuts?
Wisdom and childhood move in measure, ringed.
Lose one, then both misstep, and no birds sing.

**The Dead Find Ways to Share Their Death
(Matthew 2: 13-20)**

The dead find ways to share their deaths, with arms
outstretched; like Herod, bent on history's
brief page, they murder themselves a name, still warm
the ages: Hitler's stars, the mystery
of Rachel's children—in womb or out. We find
the dead surround us, eat our lunches, collect
our pay. Though we have never killed, nor pined
for solutions, we murder others to win respect.
Let the Mercy that quickens, wake me, save my weak
and leaning good; let Joseph make me a stand.
Let Herod, who dies too slowly in me, speak
no more, his boils become deserted sand.
A Jewish lament gives time its eternal pace.
It's the death of Jesus we hear in our Master's race.

**For Madonna House Artists
(Matthew 2: 21-23)**

In Nazareth, the drudgery of rote
is unlearned: we find our way through work, in friends.
Each sacrifice made, each small cross borne is a mote
of testimony which tells us—what could offend
more than hesitant hands? So let Joy reveal
Himself as He wills then. We will learn as we must,
to live in hidden days, in a cranking reel
by an opened window, where, as gladsome dust,
we ply our trades, weave each alleluia
to sighs, trading our time for a place; the shapes,
a noisy junket of kazoos and pennants because
we can: praising God in a swirl of capes.
In art we take His Hands, each moment's loss,
and find the joy in our waiting: Pentecost.

In the Madness of Sanity
(Matthew 3: 1-6)

In the madness of sanity, John, half-naked, hair-
shirted, speaks with the voice of the Desert Flame
who allows the grass to wither, demands men bear
the weight they've given, in pride and deeds, their names.
"Prepare the way. For what is close at hand
burns." And the people, convicted, edge in a mass
toward the bar. The Baptist would drown each man
again and again, until, in death, the last
deception goes down, and sin, our daily bread,
is exposed: a food that starves, a meal that feeds
itself. When I hear I fast, am wracked and led
to a desert, scored with personal habits, needs.
To kill this self, I need to raze what seems:
each carefully vaulted wall, each decentered beam.

This Brood of Vipers, Fleeing the Coming Fall
(Matthew 3: 7-12)

This brood of vipers, fleeing the coming fall,
are torn between the need they own, and the fee
they charge to get there. They wear their gifts for all
to see, these would-be limbs on Abraham's tree.
But John doesn't compromise with the usual reign.
Shouting loudly enough to be heard, he rails
against the lies which make of every Cain,
a neighbor, of each good will, a feeling jail.
Mercy, You walk the way each sinner chooses.
Create us again, goad us into yoke;
relieve the stone in man, in our lies, ruses;
have on us, cover our hidden sins with your cloak.
Though Mercy contains it, Justice can walk alone.
We go in twos and survive Him, stone on stone.

The Physics of Eucharist
(Matthew 3: 13-17)

To raise the earth to sacrament He ties
Himself to the homeless face. And from that wired
city of eyes, He scatters the wealthy, the wise,
calls each crippled soldier to choose his hire.
And John

        —perhaps he saw the Temple rend;
then a quantum leap: the Christ, eclipsing death,
rising, as the merely ordered shroud descends;
then disciples, eating His Body, breathing His Breath—

watches the water part, His arms on His chest,
a Voice above that paten, in rocks, echoing:
"Here dies the rest of the poor," all wrongs redressed
in the will of God, in the brokenness that brings.
I would learn submission, the loss of valued friends,
my sense of who's poor, the need for a worthy end.

Men Fast to Burn Away Their Appetites
(Matthew 4: 1-4)

"Men fast to burn away their appetites,
to make Another the centerpiece of their lives,
to move the locus of need one inch to the right.
They deny themselves, and hope, in death, to survive.
But why do You fast? To try on hunger's need,
to take man's bridle, to mouth his tired bit?
Will You become Your own dark night, will You feed
on the loss so You almost know the faith of it?
Get real. Affirm matter, which from Wisdom sprung.
That's why You came, isn't it? To make food a sign.
So do like she'll tell You. What's a few stones among
friends? Bread or wine, it all gets left behind...
In what jail is this facet of truth I speak a crime?"
"Oh taste and see...the law is food Divine."

It Could Have Been in St. Peter's Square
(Matthew 4: 5-7)—for Gore Vidal

It could have been in St. Peter's Square, a lousy
Pope on either wing. Or perhaps in Mecca,
or in the final days, believers, too drowsy
to sing: who He was sent for, trying to check
Him. Hackneyed devils bringing what they bring.
"We know Your Name, we know what You will do:
defeat the elements, flaying Yourself, oh King,
atoning for puppets.... Please do, generous ewe.
Your bleating fouls a stage You've made! And Your law!
A joke! Jump off, angels will guard Your feet
with their clucks! Why even I would offer a paw
to protect my Maker, now part of creation, sweet."
"Vision's a canker to those who think they see.
As gods they narrow, yet never cease to be."

It's Not Much, I Know
(Matthew 4: 8-11)

"It's not much, I know, what with slums and the dubious types
who eat at the better tables. Still one can whine
forever, can't one? Take what comes when it's ripe,
I say. Pleasure's no evil if seen as a sign
that life is good. There is an ease one can find
in this place: the limited joys that come with largesse.
I've come to like it, a shock, perhaps from a mind
once filled with higher saws. Welcome...to 'The Best
We Can Do.' Allow me to pour you a middling sherry.
The decanter is chipped, but the maids here are lively, can laugh.
And if you'll allow, performers will keep us merry.
I'll call for a tweedler, one who knows his craft."
"You serve yourself at table, you eat your tail.
My lovers reach, even now, for the wood, for the nails."

It's a Dark Mimesis, Death
(Matthew 4: 12-17)

It's a dark mimesis, Death. Seeing, he prods
with what seems a foot. He asks for the Baptist, makes
him John the less too soon, this mime of God,
trumped spade. He imitates sleep, but never wakes.
Look! As shadow he brings the Man, a band
of funny Galileans, and more of the lost
in Capernaum, little ditzes, building on sand.
Who else but God would choose such layered dross?
And our sin, like Naphtale's, starts to fall by degrees,
though we Jungian Shadows of Death unclench our wills
so slowly you'd think that darkness charged a fee!
What's death when it dies on every southern sill?
Mr. Death is a shade whose song is not his own.
He takes the sun's, leaves it singing to bone.

What Was It That Drew Him?
(Matthew 4: 18-22)

What was it that drew Him? Andrew and Simon, their backs
working the present, intense in their fish through strife;
not ambitious, but violent as they attacked
the bait: their song, for the nets of eternal life?
And then the apposite pair: these saplings, John
and James, nets not yet thrown, under their master's
eye, the not-quite-ready, hurried along
by the Hand which will feed them—souls: a mercy past
good sense. And Zebedee, left in the rocking boat;
not alone, because his sorrow had come. His sons
would leave the known for their lives, for the Truth who spoke
the world again: "Messiah" had begun.
Any man would follow, or give his sons in his stead.
They would walk with angels, add grief to his dying bed.

Who Can Hear This?
(Matthew 4: 23-25)

Who can hear this? He seemed to proclaim himself
as news; not indirectly as most do, but boldly
and in works: the littered sin, our garden's pelf,
no longer rejected, but raised with ease from the moulds,
as amid excited screams, disturbed wonder
even the dead were given life at His breath,
His word. And the law we thought we knew, sundered
by disciples who'd loose the phylacteries of death.
From ten towns, barren rabbis, the hungry came,
and then into synagogues where He spoke like no
one else had, the Torah. The learned, first drawn by His fame,
hung slack-jawed, fed by the harvest they'd labored to sow.
His speech, which He is, offers us life, our God.
But then He's gone, and we're left with His absence: a rod.

Father Pelton, My Spiritual Director
(Matthew 5: 1-5)

Littleness, the house where the poorest live—so small
it doesn't exist; even loneliness has gone,
those rags that undressed him. With chastened tongue he calls
down heaven, delights in being its useless pawn.
I can see clear to Jesus when he speaks:
translucent skeins of syllables, parted by God.
It's where He dwells: at the low end of meek.
(He'll inherit the earth he's left, this brother of sod!)
A poustinik, he mourns for the roots of sin
he alone discerns, assisting the hobbled he sends.
He runs, like Paul, a race, but not just to win;
because sinners don't die here, nor losing ever end.
Jesus, open this wound; complete what you start.
I waste in recycled sin, a satisfied heart.

**Happy the Child—Thérèse's Little Way
(Matthew 5: 6-8)**

Happy the child who seeks a righteousness
that's not his own. He knows his tailored place
by the crosses, which always come in local dress:
the graces he can't draw, but needs to trace.
Happy, his spirit's home is on Mercy's knee,
he whom Love wounds, tears big as peonies.
(Their cloak covers Bishops for the See
of Peter. They guard the ruled in rectories.)
Happy and pure, his bop is wafer thin;
he works his bones because he enjoys the noise,
all that crazy motion, a teapot tempest in
a clatter of piety. May he see her joy.
Walking with angels, a calliope of praise,
he pipes a merry round of mistaken days.

Happy the Peaceful Makers
(Matthew 5: 9-12)

Happy the peaceful makers, their little songs
would make Him new, to themselves firstly. They need
to see Him again in roses, need to belong
to Joy, to wrestle with language, limping, yet freed
from self-absorption: those half-constructed words
spoken in nearby rooms; from that life of delay,
where nothing is ever heard except the purge
of rueful laughter, the scourge of meted days.
They want to learn to rejoice when counted worthy
of words they have never spoken, because they know
the slugs they are, the saints they would like to be,
charged as they've been, with the urgency of the slow.
They will be the prophets' footstools, their shoulders, rests.
Gerasim will call them "Tolstoy," "Little Guests."

For My Wife, Linda
(Matthew 5: 13-16)

Salt does not reach; the stars already own
those places. It's the commonest mineral, works best
unnoticed, eclipsed. Ground in winter, it is honed,
intractable. Salt is all shield without a crest.
The man who strives past station is left with none.
He must be overlooked, or he is a spice
without a table, but nothing else: a run
at what is, missing the seasons, homey as rice.
So let the salted shine, like a hilltop lamp,
like nothing else in Galilee. Let them sing
their children's songs: stockings, soiled and damp
by the door, days which only the days can bring.
Salt belongs to the earth, but the world knows better.
Salt does its job, in a spirit that spells the letter.

Our Mother, Teresa, Lived Her Life Like This
(Matthew 5: 33-37)

Our Mother, Teresa, lived her life like this,
her "Yes," larger than speech. But we saw and were called
by what she would also say, this world's abbess,
loving Calcutta because it was the fall.
"No" was absence, so she took no note. There were
the dying to wash, the dead with TVs, alone
in their prosperity, that hackled cur
who dogs our money as if it were spiritual bone.
Empty of judgment, her mind became a place
for angels, her affirmation, a door for the poor.
In her we saw our God's Albanian face.
We could stable there, near the Wounded Heart she bore.
Self-consciousness had no place in her daily rounds;
she wanted Jesus to be both fore and ground.

We Are the Knights of Imagined Slights
(Matthew 5: 38-42)

We are the knights of imagined slights. (To quote Twain:
most tragedies never happen!) Rather, we're bared
by each contrary soul we meet, each permitted pain
because we don't recognize the faces God wears.
"If you counter ideas, don't counter the man you see.
He is God's word," Krishna, armed, might tell us.
"Don't resist the man or his humanity,
but kill without passion because you too are dust."
And my heart would be a road all walk on, my cheek,
each's every way. Christian drinks from this well,
until robbed of his place, in front of the almost-meek,
and then he stands, convicted by what he sells.
I get sent back so often you'd think I'd learn
to camp by the stile, give up each promising turn!

Forget the Law and Live It
(Matthew 5: 43-48)

Forget the law and live it, or, better, run
for joy because you can. "God's ways" will fade
like morning's respectable air. A total sun
will shine on a face simplicity has made.
Let the work of dishonest men rumble past you
with their engines; you have nothing they'd want to steal.
They are you in better clothes. Love them, each new
and cluttered landscape, the banes which keep you real.
Talk to Blake beneath his window, share your zeal
with a man who hasn't learned a thing in years,
who loves Perfection and waits for that Hand to steal
each apparent victory, loss, whatever is dear.
Our spheres of influence grow as our plans recede,
as we claim our stake in the Heart which gives us need.

The Faithful Should Work
(Matthew 6: 1-6)

The faithful should work inside a closet of bone.
They should inspect their hands in the morning light,
get used to the wrinkles, learn to call them home.
How else will they ever hope to get it right?
It's easy to think that we are nobody's pawns:
we walk in the light, after all, of the Holy See.
But the hairs of self-promotion are counted on
ours heads; each speaks of our duplicity.
So where can we find wardrobes deep enough
to find us missing, yet living abundant lives?
How can we be bold enough to carry each cuff,
each angry flaw, our lonely midnight drives?
We've got to go when we know we can never be true.
To tell the Truth, a terrible thing to do.

Like Tiny Clams, Seeds Open in Darkness
(Matthew 6: 7-15)

Like tiny clams, seeds open in darkness, reveal
the extent of their need, each bent little cry, God knows
alive on His doorstep, each movement His own as He peels
the self with its mask so that tender shoots can grow.
And language flowers, beneath the Hand which begins
all things, out of void, miraculous, a prayer
which is His Word, written in grass and fin:
the Eucharist finally—God, and the only way there.
And then we're free to ask for earthly bread,
for the grace to live a simple life. His hand
fashions, as He asks for foolish hearts, treads
us, burghers, back to the plow, opening land.
Forgiveness cracks us, wide as the Father's heart.
Open, and your well-made plans start coming apart.

**For Father Callahan, Madonna House Priest
(Matthew 6: 16-18)**

We need two faces, a double chin, one pair
of eyes to watch the other wince, to ignore
that pain, his stamps and whistles, his final glare
as the better us stands guard, a smile at the door.
But our dying half may not want to play, to stay
in the crypt. A boot may recall a trace of moan,
the mission far behind the voice, the way
I remembered his almost silent gift, which honed
him until he died, a living sacrifice
of praise as he carried another's burden behind
the gravel, the measured words, paying the price
of the cross as he'd talk or fish, a hollowing rind.
The giants who go before us we seldom see.
They've lost themselves in the masses at Calvary.

For Eleanora Holiday
(Matthew 6: 19-21)

To live where our treasure is, where we'd like to be
doesn't sound much like a Herculean task.
The blues are better there; the toast, the tea.
But something in us requires revelry, a masque:
the mundane hours perhaps, the two-faced mirror.
We want Southampton's art, Bacon's scope,
more rooms so we won't see our cabin stir.
We don't want to be found here, victims of stagnant hope.
But those sloughs of despond are where we become our need,
because you can't tell who's faithful until winds blow,
until, in snow, you must wait for the splitting seed,
God dancing so slowly it seems He'll never show.
Spiritual death is ugly. Why shouldn't it be?
It's a ripening Fruit, strange, on a distant tree.

St. Catherine of Siena and the "Other"
(Matthew 6: 22-23)

The jaundiced eye, it distorts to avoid that toad,
life. To see would bruise the ego, to take
one's place on a faceless penitential road.
But this "other" had a self, a niche to make.
And if what was real had to die for him to get
the reaction he wanted, he'd use that loss to beat
his friends, the Fellowship. Feeding on holy regret,
she'd pay for the love he offered, its languished heat.
And they did suffer, because he never quite sensed
the leer behind his grin. In quiet, subdued
quasi-Christian letters penned from his bench,
he chose a hell over the people he knew.
Deciding on distance, he'd dangle just out of reach;
a puppet showing his strings—like a day at the beach.

Feed Your Poems to the Birds
(Matthew 6: 25-34)

Let me feed my cares to birds; if I make them bread,
they will eat. Otherwise they'll do no good,
either to me or the stories I walk in. Instead,
let me work in palimpsest, in the leisure which stood
with Twain as, like Huck, he rafted, each new river
a Mississippi, just a pole, calm stars
to wile away the catfish nights, a sliver
of moon, cabin's lantern beyond the bar.
He added the tar, of course, the king, the duke.
He made up every day then night of rain.
Leisure's tramp, he tried each puddle, his flukes,
because he saw the world in Grandma's lane.
Wear the warm air, lilies will be your staff.
Playful worms will scratch you an epitaph.

Old Habits Are Tough to Break
(Matthew 7: 1-5)

Old habits are tough to break, tickering parades,
because who else can come so close to the mind
of God? I'm the product of youthful barricades:
vanity, my defense against absent parents I pined
for. Even now, I cattle myself, believe
that only an ignorant man would fall in a ditch
of his own making. A spiritual Mitty, I'm deceived
by the burden of perfect judgment, my ark's dark pitch.
Prayer's the answer, of course. It's always been.
But how can I deflate complacency
when Walter crowds me on buses, borrowing pens,
passing gossip that begins and ends with me?
I'd throw up my hands, but that is not allowed.
So I walk Confessional, meek, head mostly bowed.

We Live in Two Faces
(Matthew 7: 6)

We live in two faces, though one you cannot see;
that world, an invisible oyster, sporting pearls
from no sea. And though this kingdom is yet to be,
I stand erect, try to keep my flagging furled,
for we serve, you see, an exacting absent Lord.
And though I know I'll never be worthy to trod
this path, nor can I count the cache I've stored,
I beat the only, the narrow way to God.
It's crazy, materialists say: this nosing the air,
sniffing for scentless clues, pretending my lot
makes me better, saintly, set apart, like some rare
and bloodless species, they a doggy blot.
This "chosen" bit can snag. What can we do?
Limp on, until they see the other shoe.

The Other World Is One of Plenty
(Matthew 7: 7-11)

The other world is one of plenty, with ripe
answers for our questions which drop from the vine.
It's a world I know, where the choirs, the throated pipes
of lilies finish each partially scripted line.
It's where I'm called, in joy, beyond the "here,"
where what is real seldom happens, as far
as the eye can see. It's where the Answer's so near
I walk It, like wise men calling down the star.
It's madness to live where Jesus is, in the spring
of what's yet fully to be, where the asked-for fast
from sin and food makes stone-hearted Abrahams sing.
Touched by heaven's reach, I exceed my grasp.
To be a fool like the world had never seen;
so Francis was, but the place was always green.

Gamaliel's Rule
(Matthew 7: 12)

Jesus lifted this one, though He thought of it first,
since all of truth emanates from a God
who breathes this world alive; whose ploughing bursts
through sod, as down our sillions we trod.
For who of us can own virtue, decree
what erodes our poses, bit by blessed bit?
When zealot Paul says "It's Christ who lives in me,"
it's not hyperbole. God has found him fit
for dress. As man Paul's dust again, like before
his turn—now he gives the very life he sought!
And this is where I stick: that at my core
I matter so much less than I had thought.
But in God's sight I am golden, flesh and tooth,
a boast from One who can only speak the truth.

On God, Who Writes Straight With Crooked Lines
(Matthew 7: 13-14)

The gate is Confessional thin, more narrow within.
I follow, gracefully awkward. A sign of the cross
marks me. Then a priest's insight, outside the din
of the media world, measures what I've lost.
And though a prodigal joy lights up heaven,
here I hack worn paths, proceed with what passes for speed,
getting correctional glimpses of Will, leaven
for my faulty resolve which dampens in my need
for the infantile: hanging drunk from window seats,
or chasing the chase, a momentary bliss.
Expending spirit, checking the times for the heat,
I want the action's action, its final kiss.
The road to heaven is heaven, all the saints say;
it's less-traveled by because so much of it strays.

Though Cults Use the Name of Jesus
(Matthew 7: 15-20)

Though cults use the name of Jesus to hook the sheep,
Catholics seldom do. We'll mention Christ
now and again, as prelude to talk of deep
spiritualities, liturgies, given our Zeitgeist.
But perhaps that shouldn't surprise. Look at this world,
where nothing we see is ever as it seems:
the beautiful woman, controlled, while her string of pearls
is trampled by pigs, who root her fields for dreams.
To see the fruit of action we must be still
long enough to let the personae play it out.
A maker's vision comes after the players' bill
is paid, and hands close on the last bowing lout.
False prophets hide in a tree of catholic sense,
each act rich with a cognoscente's pence.

We Hear the Wisdom of God
(Matthew 7: 24-29)

We hear the wisdom of God, but how well does it take?
We'll pray for awhile. But soon we're off to the fair,
like puppies afield, until missing steps, half-awake,
we return to a milky haze for motherly care.
Stupid is, and does, and doesn't act as he should,
despite his foundation. My building skills are what
is at question: my mortar mix, the bow in my wood.
Windows fall out, and my door, like my mouth, won't shut.
What will I do when my Lord returns? Offer snails,
mutter about the sea, my hitching thumb?
Will I claim, "Master, I only knew how to fail
when You pulled me from the song of passing rum"?
No, I'll fall on my wayward Christian face,
wait without options, in sinful silence—for grace.

Francis' Leper
(Matthew 8: 1-4)

Some cures seem to take longer: prayer, a fast,
which would almost get me down to my proper weight.
If I want to be cured so badly, why does the past
smother the need, lead me with factious bait?
To deliver that sanguine virtue, humility?
The only virtue found in its absence! No doubt.
Though I know he'd rather hang with people who see
more of the Truth, those with some holy clout.
He'll get here, I know, though it might take him some years
what with all that ritual cleansing he'll have to do
(giving me time to cow my childish fears,
to learn to separate my sin from the view).
I'd gladly show the priests what's become of me,
if I could calm and win that leprosy.

Jesus, Amazed
(Matthew 8: 5-13)

Jesus, amazed. And yet how could that be so?
Did He walk blind, in Love, so that we might see
Him restore the house of time; so that we might know
how small our benches are, how absurd our decrees.
"Life is huge," He tells us with capacious voice:
His words scaffold heaven, that fierce kingdom
that comes, on the wake of every freeing choice,
where what was lived for is finally, terribly, done.
This Centurion, pawn, killer of Jews, didn't bribe
the Truth! It came! Perhaps through slaves' gossip,
gleanings from the fringes of a stiff-necked tribe,
from zealots, who'd pray while they were being whipped.
When Authority spoke, he knew enough to hear.
It seldom had to, what with its armies near.

The Jokes Come Easy Here
(Matthew 8: 14-15)

The jokes come easy here; the only way
He could stop her from complaining was to heal
her latest cause. But she doesn't get that say.
This lamb, whom Peter would leave, prepares a meal.
Healing wounds so old they've become cliché,
He opens scions, bids fruit come bud in Him.
But whatever became of her, did she replay
the scenes long after, her life, by then, a hymn?
Did she feel confirmed at unsurprising news,
God still, and always, followed by backward man?
Did she foreknow the first martyrs from the pew
of her kitchen window, each lover of Truth's last stand?
Our lives are like laundry, hung in an empty sky,
as Jesus prepares, through the years, our waiting eyes.

The End As Photograph
(Matthew 8: 16-17)

This was not the pompadour right, no sleight-of-hand
sideshow. How rowdy things must have gotten! The hairs
on the back of the whole region's neck had to stand
on end as *all* who played were paid at this fair.
Think of the hawkers! The possibilities!
New limbs on display, the unrestrained good cheer—
though our Lord, bearing our infirmities,
publicly living His private life, had to hear
the talk: "a Davidic King," the zealots read
of Him. "But can He manipulate this renown?"
Jesus was gone before He'd learned to lead—
to the next person, banquet, piquing small town.
Three years would go fast, because the Truth won't wait.
He comes in a flash, catches the world in a state.

What Did He See in the First?
(Matthew 8: 18-22)

What did He see in the first? The blinds of ego?
A disciple asking to widen the rudder's arc?
If so, Truth gave "Noah" a corrective blow:
he who wanted to leave one, could fix on an inner mark.
And the next, was he lost in the camp-following wings?
Did he think the twinkle of gauds would help him see?
Jesus cut to the beating heart of things,
past platelet and bone, without that lie: pity.
He hadn't time, realizing each day,
bringing Narcissus to the glass, sweeping
each cottage clean. The Truth will only say
itself, not dreams. Find it, and you'll hear weeping.
Though I am slow, He never sends me away.
He gives me ears to live with the things I say.

What Do You Say When God So Shatters the Known
(Matthew 8: 23-27)

What do you say when God so shatters the known,
that you're left with nothing, shards of who you were;
not the storm, but the calm after, each of you bone
wet, left with the mast, a past that hasn't occurred?
This is how poverty starts, with just you and Him
and the flimsy material world, surrounded by souls
you know you're here for, by depths you can only skim—
a rocky night without recognizable shoals.
This is why pennies matter, on the ground.
So you can pick them up well, and be amazed
at a God who so manipulates each found
moment that work becomes a kind of play.
We know nothing beyond the God who has us here.
And duty? It sounds like jazz to wakening ears.

On a Theme Lifted from C. S. Lewis
(Matthew 8: 28-34)

They asked Him to leave! Too many pork chops and choice
spirits perhaps: a larger world, exposed
to view, with "appointed times," hellish voices.
Goods had been destroyed, ex-thugs in repose.
They didn't want that. They wanted the coins they knew,
an almost peaceful place, with Rome on edge.
It was sorrowful, yes, but the corn and the children grew.
Let those pigs be the last to test that prophet's ledge.
And what could Jesus do when fools bid Him go?
He left them to their shrinking illusion of "town."
The time is always short, and a hungry wind blows
before and after that piggy, truth, is drowned.
Without our God, we scatter back to the sea.
Pigs and people trade places, become one species.

Prayer at Fifty
(Matthew 9: 1-8)

Christ is the tense He alone creates: a present,
so alive with healing, heaven's economy
that He fences the faith of friends for the cripples bent
with paralyzed fear. "Virtue," he says, "is free."
(Teaching the moment to time, He utters Mercy,
ecce Homo, giving two hands to the good.)
But the wise men have their rules, and disagree.
Seers need a guide through a darkened wood!
And so Christ, like a teacher trained for the job, uses aids:
calls forth the child, so that even the learned might hear.
Recoiling, the oldest lies begin their fade;
new faces are born, as Heaven Itself draws near.

But how can I keep Him, this God who gives such joy?
I've shoeboxes, pockets, the spotted hands of a boy.

Matthew Was in the Counting House
(Matthew 9: 9)

Matthew was in the counting house, counting
on vacations—the days away from minding the sore.

The sky was blue, so he lunched outside, mounting
with birds who returned, too soon, to the dying shore.

But then that voice! Like living internal waters,
it startled alive the sea of its promise: life!

His futures vanished like the shams they were,
as he quit his job—for abstractions, a heavenly fife!
It made him laugh. There might be dues, but he'd pay
for his choice because what could he lose but this mangy fleece
called life? The world could take it every day:
a coat that would wear you, down, its own police.

Unless we are called, how can we come up chosen?
We'd sit between movements, never put our toes in.

**Matthew Was Stunned to See
(Matthew 9: 10-13)**

Matthew was stunned to see his part of town
so transformed: with rabbis, women of the night.
This Jesus wasted no time in bringing down
their noses, to smells more real than "spiritual blight."
"Yes, inhale, my brothers, because who can tell
what sways each viper's nest, the human heart....

And how will I know this master's vision from hell
if his only guide is a sorcerer's personal art?...

But that voice! It comes from a different country, a place
where mercy abides, where scribes are made to kneel....

But can this radical shift leave a lasting taste?...

Well, prison always ends with a last good meal."

Humility was the only, and sane way to go.
He knew that, but not how far he'd have to row.

God Honors What He's Made: the Exertion of Sweat (Matthew 9: 14-17)

God honors what He's made: the exertion of sweat,
sustained. Like call and response in church or jazz,
the human gets to work with God, who lets
the dialogue happen in fallen time. It's as
little Thérèse once told me, lifting her shift
to turn: "Yes, I have done this," her life, a bold
template, challenging me to brave the rift,
as if prayer, an alembic, could turn my copper to gold.
My will is weak—old fiber, shrunken cloth,
too frayed to hold a stitch. So I welcome her hand,
will try to be open to every passing moth
(to holes which widen as my prospects expand).
Thérèse, if you take my hand, I'll be your child:
I'll walk beside clicking beads, in single file.

The Flutists Were Wrong
(Matthew 9: 18-26)

The flutists were wrong! And if they were wrong about death,
they were wrong about everything else. And so are we.
We don't know life, nor God, nor why we are left
feeling stranded, without an anchoring sea.
How could we know less? Oh, we march around with our canes,
gesticulating, buying and selling goods
which are the flotsam of lives nearly lived, a strained
bluster, to keep our bearings, what's understood.
The crone, though, knew what only those who feed
on suffering can: that insistent flesh is a rod.
And appearances? For dandies, fops. Real need
drove her to crawl on the ground to a passing God.
Complacent wisdom, at end, will get put out.
Let my soul walk raw, in the elements of doubt.

Since No One Could See Them
(Matthew 9: 27-31)

Since no one could see them, the blind men didn't care.
With walking sticks against the only night,
off-hands, awkwardly reaching for God in the air:
they called and their futures rose, met their Sight....
Like new coins, these eyes!...And all they'd felt, they now
could touch!...Jesus tried to keep them in line,
because they didn't know Whom to praise. They bowed,
then fought to settle in, these heavenly signs.
But a red sun saucered the water—aflame!
Like kids sprung on school's last day, they hopped
and rammed into one another, each wanting to claim
this road. Christ smiled. Who knew when they'd stop?
Deferring, Jesus wanted the incense to rise.
And the Father? He'd given the Spirit Mary's eyes.

A Set of Propositions
(Matthew 9: 32-34)

"A set of propositions: start with the known.
One: 'We are right.' Therefore you're allowed no name
of your own. Contingent, you will have to roam
until settled. Say, if you must, the Sanhedrin's to blame.

Two: 'What we don't know yet, won't be revealed.'

Three: 'God works through us.' And why not? We're tall
and learned. We've earned the right, come up with a seal.
Someone has to do this. Think of it as a call."

And so the Pharisee is the center, and all
gets turned around. Black becomes white, and noise
becomes sound. It's the nagging sin that shapes our fall.
We've never hit ground. We just keep on falling through toys.
Evil is subtle as an evening breeze:
tiny yeses, to any lie you please.

He Was God, but Bound by Two Hands
(Matthew 9: 35-38)

He was God, but bound by two hands, He couldn't reach:
all the people harassed by lies which feed on our lives,
every packaged demand for money's deserted beach,
the hope that won't come until the goods arrive.
Their means were limited, resources nearly the same,
these hatchlings, already reaching for their Host.
So He became our Bread—without limbs, for the lame;
God's voice, without one: heaven's only boast.
And because only a child can open those doors,
as wide as God, a hush still settles the man
who visits, bowed, his face to the marble floor.
We receive our reply: a piece of the primal plan.
Prayer makes the long-awaited harvest rich.
We ask in an answer, wait in vain for a hitch.

This Is the Lion's Mouth
(Matthew 10: 1-16)

"This is the lion's mouth, and here his teeth....
Bring back the dead, be poor.... Take My power
and use it.... I'll raise a repentant Sodom, beneath
sword and thigh, to vanquish his final hour."
Who ever spoke like this? Like the world was His own.
This was no holy man who'd toured the East,
and, enlightened, used its skill to riddle koans.
No, He spoke like His word had sounded beasts,
had given nature a way, each pupil an eye.
He spoke, not about what might occur, but of things
that would happen because He spoke them—in the face of lies:
freedom sold to license, a sword for its sting.
May the Lord be pleased to tender our serpentine way,
as He flutes us, doves, builds the house of our praise.

You'll Meet With Kings
(Matthew 10: 17-25)

You'll meet with kings. And then dropping the other shoe:
their swords. This is how badly people want truth—
who is a good dog until she crosses you.
Then she's put down, for a necklace, a devil's tooth.
All part of the irrevocable plan of God.
He gives us speech, another world, which might
appear to those on the fence an unseemly rod
since it spares the enemy, his encroaching night.
But we're only traveling here. We're the baggage we bear
as we write the truth in dust, on pilgrim feet.
We're called to detach ourselves from the cautious care
we give, to our enemies, to these tangled streets.
We could be waiting for a bus, or tea.
Hope like a votive flickers. We rock in this sea.

Moments of Conscience
(Matthew 10: 26-33)

It's the extent of the sin that gets them. Saints learn
who they are in a sure darkness; all their lives,
praying for the grace that unnerves them: unearned
moments of conscience. Isn't that what we strive
for: to find the porch of our beginnings, coming
out or in? And our God, doesn't He dance
most cleanly among what's broken: in the dark, offering
what we don't value: the sparrow's song, repentance,
everything dun-colored, small.
                           Our gut
must convict us, in each unspoken denial:
in all of what we don't say, and in most of what
we do. Our badges, lies, must taste like bile.
John Vianney asked God to show him his every sin;
weeks later, he stopped up his ears against the din.

As We Age, We Must Hurry to Gall Ourselves
(Matthew 10: 34-36)

As we age, we must hurry to gall ourselves, be stout:
like bundles of sticks standing against—the flames.
We must be pure verb as we burn each virtue out,
Catherines of Siena, take the blame
when momentum fails, our lives now at a stake.
We need to unsettle ourselves in the extreme,
cut each societal bond: uncles making
nephews, a daughter-in-law's replenished dream.
Here, in the very place that offers us rest,
we must find none. We serve in these houses because
we pass our own like ships in the fight; "our" "nest"
is neither. And our resolve? A piffle, a pause.
If we don't drive ourselves, we will in the end,
up Dante's mountain, with all our lighthouse friends.

No Home Is Ours
(Matthew 10: 37-39)

No home is ours, either when we were kids
or now. As parents, though we fret in our watch,
we fail. And which of our sins will shape the skids
of their future years? Under their eyes, each botch;
our "hearts" see all.... But must I be at their beck
and call, pay for each fault: father as fodder,
as I try to eclipse my past? Must I now reck
two rods—they'd make impossibly urgent Gods!

Our crosses are always us, what we drag through the pews
of our despond. Childhood's perpetual demands
still flay us: poor men's St. Bartholomews—
while our wives work until they can barely stand.
A household's a joyful crucible where we die
too slowly, and get to know the reasons why.

It's Better to Be a Clear Lens
(Matthew 10: 40-42)

It's better to be a clear lens than to die
chasing the prophet's timeless pose. Here He
is just the Word, never drawing our eyes
to His person. He's not some nova, just His speech,
actions. Picasso would've been appalled:
a genius who didn't live to preen
before the crowds each painter works to stall,
a Byron who wouldn't vent his golden spleen
before the camera of literary
history. And to make sure we don't drown
out those disciples more notable than we,
he folds us, "little" sheep, so we can't expound.
Lord, let us circle You, the dimmest of stars,
so removed that only You see who we are.

Feasting With Hookers, Tax Men
(Matthew 11: 1-15)

Feasting with hookers, tax men—upon what scrolls
was *this* written? And if on theirs, then why
wasn't he told? Was he on these prison rolls
for instructing God's only people in how to lie?

Christ tells His prophet to stand down, to know
less: people were being healed, posturing spurned;
the seeds of the Father's love were being sown.
(Even the holiest can stop and learn!)

Then facing His cross, His heart, Christ waters the Baptist,
names him Elijah—though every prophet pales
in the penumbra of heaven, where the missed
and forgotten trade their successes for a sail.

Christ is a song that no one else can sing:
Our vowels don't open; our kites tangle our string.

Driving Next to My Down's Son, Jude
(Matthew 11: 25-30)

Driving next to my Downs son, Jude, I say,
"You know, I'm really not very learned." He replies:
"Me neither, Dad." He is a prophet, his days,
a struggle to find humility's proper size.
He is the road his father must learn to walk:
living in the present: facing his fears.
His speech is impeded, yes, but I've learned to chalk
that up to the good: we all must stop to hear!
He has West Virginia playing the Seahawks, sock
cousins, and if he pushes his play past
good sense, it's because he's so eager, so locked
into his "Yes"—the fun goes by too fast!
The Father swims in the strokes of His eager Son.
He races with Him until time itself is undone.

Lyrics

(For Scott Robinson's Christian
Sufi Band, Mandala)

Hide and Seek
(Madonna House: Ontario)

Holy One, You cannot hide.
Chopping frozen wood, I see You,
imbedded above my breath and sweat,
in the late morning above-the-western-trees
razor blue sky.

You laugh,
You sit on punctual pines where snow
gathers so graciously to the ground;
on bushes, pounds of thick sculpted hats,
shifting shawls, the stinging beads
of white.

You lurk amid the red hair of the birch
(a pure mutiny!), in new water where,
more than once, I've addled in my canoe.

I could tell everyone,
but this cold trumpet, this bright note,
how can I play it
until You stop singing?

Our Father

Glory to the Father
who guideth His children with a tender hand,
who watches over the hay-bailers,
and to Whom the cricket sings.
He is like the stars and the broad rivers
that move beneath them.
He is like Paris or Rome.
He is like taxes.

He forgeth the metal in the fire,
the birds fly from His singing,
glows at the end of the day.

Who is there to visit Him?
Who to bring Him mirrors?

Hyperbole

Praise the Lord
who loveth the fat man,
for he is jocund,
who loveth the beetle and the amoeba
for they are universes
unto themselves,
who maketh the round ball
and the skinny hole.

He is the milk and sap
of our dispositions, the red arm,
the other shoe. We walk
for hours behind Him,
losing our way,
losing our way.

PSALMS

Psalm #1

He does not linger with scoffers
in the slow swirl,
bubbled stem of settled
bar beer, the loiterers'
golden climb.

He sweats all day in Presence,
mumbles among his tools.

How could he be moved?
He is the original natural man;
his laugh, the laugh of water.

Not so the wicked, not so.
He has no self
outside of God, sees what he is
as drives, no one behind the wheel;
chaff, before too many winds.

So how shall he stand—then?

The way of the wicked
is too wide for signposts.
It is a desolate field
and offers the nothing
no one can take.

Psalm #4

When have You not come?
You are corn and wine, honey
on the tongue, like bees.

Hear me.

You men—and me,
why shut your hearts and not your mouths,
loving delusion, what fades:
the silk in mist?

Know this idolaters—my heart,
Yahweh has already
given what you need:
in the fierce conscription of stars,
the slow corsage of night:
coal barges, their wake and wash
along the river's shore.

Yahweh leaves a full heart at night
(my young family upstairs),
a sigh which is gratitude,
a little rain,
and then sleep.

Psalm #5

Like a deer or its hunter,
You watch for me each morning
in the twigs,
in the whole earth
which rises through wetness,
sleep.

I ready myself
in the discipline of a supplicant.

Hear me.

Your favor covers the virtuous man.

Let me walk upright
clad in Your sun, high days,
my spear in hand.
Let a riot of flowers attend me:
little soldiers, strong-stemmed,
with their laughter, their opened,
now-here,
now-there faces.

Psalm #6

Do not punish me, do not
stamp my soul with the seal
of who I am.
Lift me up and I will rise,
pity me, I cannot keep
my bones, the rack
upon which I starve, knit.

Come back, rescue me.
This is what You do.

I could sing Your praises
in the lands of the dead,
but who would hear me?
Take these hands, lifted;
a person follows.

I am worn out with groaning,
my enemies, younger each year,
surround me.

Yahweh calls me back
as he always has,
with the sound of trumpets,
the breaking of expected days.

I come,
in human skin.

Psalm #7

Yahweh, if I am to die,
let it be in the sweet scythe
of Your wood.
Rise, You Who demand
justice bear Your name.
Look past intention.
Look at this face, a cooling fire,
these hands, crumbling
winter leaves.

God preserves what He has pierced.

Give thanks to Yahweh,
whose voice creaks
in the starry wood,
the whole place alive, somehow,
with water. Heavy grasses,
green, dark with it,
and I feel the same night
the foliage does,
recite the same verses;
my body, too, belonging
to the great material curve
of this planet, sky.
It is who I am, this way and
terminus. It haunts
my every blind and
faithful step
with the signature
of what we are, the promise
of where we live.

Psalm #8
(apologies to Catullus)

When I sit under stars,
a necklace of cold soldiers
You have set in place,
I ask, what is man
that You should save his smile?

You, who have put fields of this dark stuff,
moist dirt in our hands!
And beasts! Huge flanked thugs,
hope on the hoof—the Catholic Farm!
Being bounced around by cows:
scattering potato halves
from a bushel basket.

Life, like a noisy engine,
forces its way out everywhere:
hair growing out of my ears at night,
whispering their dark glyphs to me
as I sleep.

How raucous is Your name, Lord.
Who could pronounce It?
In swirls of dust, rumor it comes,
in a scare of buffalo,
ground shaking under hoof,
clumps of sod everywhere.

Someone is going to have to clean that up.

Psalm #42

In the woods,
behind a dark tangle,
the blackened arms of trees,
in the deer's rhythmic,
bough-like chew, its hooves,
moves the cold creak of the stream.

Moon overhead,
and through the rakes of trees
drift the parched, wasted
corn stalks, the snow clouds.

A colder wind calls
through wet, slacking limbs.
My hands clam deep in the soil,
fingers pressed years
beneath the earth.
My head hangs like a gourd.

I meet You, in the red
veins of the beets,
Indian arrowheads, winging
geese. And at night, in the stars,
the slow sway in the tall thicket,
the blue moon
and first broad flakes.

Psalm #44

All day long I brood over this,
draw Your dark numbers.
My life, either death or death:
the slow interminable wait,
the death of license,
the rage between them.
And like Peter, to whom
shall I turn?

I've heard the voices, every one:

"If the moment does not scald us,
we are not in it."

"If our lives do not take us,
where then is the giving?"

If I forget You, wouldn't
You know it? It is
for Your sake I am,
as always, being reduced
to my sighs.
Why do You sleep? Rise up,
reach me leper, my uneven fingers
knotting,
in the dirt.

POEMS BASED ON
ST. ALPHONSE LIGUORI'S
Preparation for Death

Consideration I
Portrait of a Man who has recently gone into the Other World

"Dust thou art, and unto dust thou shalt return."
—*Gen. iii. 19*

The worms, kissing cousins
to your sewn lips
are not in denial.
They will circle your ear:
schoolboy heads, attentive,
lifted for a moment; they celebrate
a more comprehensive democracy.

And you, still on your damp bed:
hair, disordered
in a way you hoped
might save you; that bath of sweat
which did not clean; your eyes
can no longer dance
as they once did: to your advantage—
around what matters.
Your face, ashen; your furtive tongue,
almost still; body, too cold for any passage.
It, too, a kind of tongue.

And your huddled own!
Tears you would save in a vial!
But they, all of them, must leave,
their clocks, up now and running
after their own lives.

Your body has already begun its seep:
into the swampy moil, the plaguey bill.
Open the windows. Bring in some incense!
You will not be incorrupt!

> *St. Ambrose said, "If he has been one of the nobles of the
> earth, his body shall send forth a more intolerable stench."*

And so, really, how did you see yourself,
your modest, almost comfortable place?
Lies! All of them,
the goodness you carried:
the thinnest silver rose!

In time, the empty room
will be filled up again:
more odors to replace the ones
that replaced yours. Your grandchildren
will be the last to remember: more lies
than truth, everything
they needed you to be.

Lord, I am corrupted!
But tell me, wouldn't it ever be so?

> *St. Chrysostom too: "Go to the grave; contemplate
> dust, ashes, worms; and sigh."*

First you turn yellow,
like an overturned canary,
then black, they say, as the troughs
of despair you tried,
which could not feed you.
Afterwards, your fine white glove
covered in mold!

The wags of the last generation,
where are they now? Enter their apartments,
slippers they so fit.
If you wish to see them,
knock at the door of their new houses.
For all their wit,
no one followed.

And the "unfavored,"
look how *they* are housed: little tabernacles
locket the smallest shard of bone or tooth;
their hands were strangers
in front of them, their feet,
given over to paths
they had not set down.

They wasted none of the coins we get.

To be noticed was, for them,
an impediment.

    Consider yourself already dead says St. Laurence Justinian.

And if you were already dead,
what teeth would you not have cut?

When St. Camillus de Lellis saw graves, he said within
himself: if these were to return to life, what would
they not do for eternal glory?

So why do I waste the only time I get,
dragging my feet, expending effort
which might, even now,
kindle some worthier enterprise?

Remember, says St. Bernard, that the Lord seeks not only
the hesitant beauty of buds, but the real weight of fruits.

Lord, give me an ache—
deep enough to effect the way I walk.

Mary,
exalted high school barefoot Queen,
how could I ever hope to know you—
but anyway, hear the cry
I want to be.

Consideration II
With Death All Ends

> *"An end is come, the end is come."*
> —*Ezek. vii. 6*

Morning mist
like some huge, marvelous ship,
sails low through the grasses;
but even that loses its place—
to birds, backfires.

We must leave every biker's sunrise,
here, on this beautiful,
foreign plain.

> *Thomas a Kempis's brother preened over a house he had*
> *built, until a friend told him it had one great defect: a*
> *door—a door that would spit him out, helpless, that one*
> *last time, before the ways and backs of this world!*

Oh, what a fevered spectacle!
Importance banished from its own shows!

The Saladin, who had so enlarged his aura in Asia,
left one last directive: that his fleshy purse
be preceded by a flag-waver,
a winding sheet
on a hoisted maypole, announcing:
"This is what Saladin brings with him."

> *"Contemplate," St. Basil says, "the sepulchers of the*
> *dead, take away the stones, and see if you can find*
> *differences under the earth."*

Alexander noticed Diogenes
rummaging through our legacy: bones.
"I am looking for the skull of Philip.
If you can find it, show me.
I want a fit place, so all the earth will mark him."

Men, Seneca says, are born in the squalor
of chance: unequally gifted—
but that, as he points out, passes.
And Horace, he wondered why we wait
on the scepter, and not
on the more pointed spade.

All that we possess in this world
are words
and the time to deny them.

At the hour of his demise, Phillip II,
King of Spanish dirt, called his son,
and throwing off ermine, revealed
the turning (cancerous) worm:
"Prince, though your name would raise you,
know where
and with whom you shall lie!"

> *St. Antonine relates that after the death of Alexander the*
> *Great a certain philosopher exclaimed: "Behold! The*
> *man who yesterday trampled on the earth, how now he*
> *is tamped below. Yesterday the earth could not contain*
> *him, and today six men put him down."*
> *Why is earth and ashes proud?*
> *—Ecclus. x. 9.*

Why do we spend the only thoughts we get
plotting after fortune, greatness,
which, to tell the truth,
have always had their own
slightly medieval agendas?
Both idle through time
as if oblivious,
moving from flower to flower,
never once consulting us.

The world spins
through everything it carries.
Death will come; and then what good
will be the succession of houses, apartments,
which have so marked our progress?

> *In that day all their thoughts shall perish.*
> *—Ps. cxlv. 4.*

St. Paul the Hermit lived sixty years on roots—
next to Nero! And who had the better death,
St. Felix or Henry the Eighth?
Tell me, which of his wives
rose up to defend *him*?

Only the hungry are really fed in this world.

How can dandies, living for rivaled sins,
whatever good they call them,
expect a peaceful death, when diversions
will have been what they lived for?
Will they denounce their hollow victories
at closing? Will they brand themselves fools
for the benefit of those next in line?

Who could do as much?

Our hearts give table to our habits.

> *Like a dream upon waking, Lord, when you awake,*
> *you dismiss their image.*
> —*Ps. lxxii. 20.*

Happiness is a measure of sin
if it comes by grasping; it is a tincture, then,
which promises a wound!

St. Francis Borgia, accompanying the Empress
Isabella to Grenada, came alive
when they opened her coffers—coffin:
her face, a decayed mash, the smell,
so effective, it kept others running.

And who wrote those words
on a skull:
"*Cogitanti vilescunt omnia*"?

And what would *you* take
in your shabby bag?
Photos of younger people: your children—
all gone, beyond retrieval?

> *O ye sons of men, how long will you be dull of heart?*
> *Why do you love vanity, and seek after falsehood?*
> —*Ps. iv. 3.*

Why do we so love a god
who is all arms?

What has happened to our forefathers,
after all, will certainly happen to us.
They have weeded in our gardens;
they have slept in our very beds.
Turn the hoe, brother; they have done it.
Raise it high in your good effort;
they demanded as much.

And who eats so noisily at my side?

> *Whatsoever thy hand is able to do, do it earnestly.*
> *—Eccles. ix. 10.*

There is a reason why what we can do today
has come! Tomorrow
is a luxury—proposed.
And a day, once passed,
is a discredited witness, a liar
who can only call down the halls
of a banked memory.

See what is before you.

Do what you would not.

> *Blessed are the dead who die in the Lord.*
> *—Apoc. xiv. 13.*

Happy are they who, at death, can wait
for suitors. Death, a slow angel,
even she will be Sister!

Both of them, dancing haltingly,
as it were,
into the hereafter.

My Lord, take me out
before You let me linger.

Mary, my hope, school me.

Consideration III
Shortness of Life

> *"What is your life? It is vapor, which appeareth*
> *for a little while."*
> —James, iv. 15.

What is your life?
Vapor—like every friend you've ever had!

Everybody knows death
will come—but after, we hope,
we've had time to set our colleagues
straight, to position our offspring.

> *But Job tells us that the life of man is short. Man born of*
> *a woman, living for a short time...who cometh forth*
> *like a flower, and is destroyed.*

> *Isaiah, too, cried....All flesh is grass....Indeed, the people*
> *is grass. The grass is withered, and the flower is fallen.*

The life of man crawls
in the coming,
but is swifter than youth
in the winding down:
a blade of grass before "the blond assassin,"
and our green woodland
dress, our beautiful summer
is gone:
dried leaves in a vault of wind.

> *My days, says Job, have been swifter than a runner.*
> —Job, ix. 2.

Death, all dressed up,
leans against your house in tipped, bowler hat
until it's time for you
to know.

> *"What I write," says Jerome, "is time taking away my life."*

> *We all die, and, like the waters that return*
> *no more, we fall into the earth.*
> *—2 Kings, xiv. 14.*

> *And only the grave remaineth for me*
> *—Job, xvii. 1.*

We shall all be young Mozarts,
thrown into a common grave,
covered with the lime of memories—
no good to anyone now.
And the honors which promised a harvest?
Bitters, herbs we take,
at these, our final weekday meals.

Ah, how we will pine for time then:
second guesses, holistic remedies;
but we'll be cut off in mid-sentence
because death, the henchman,
the needed one,
doesn't care about our opinions.

Jesus, Lord,
how often have I preferred pleasure,
sordid, even in the taking;
judgments as if they were breath itself;
a life of caprice, high-jinx:

beer, marbles,
anything to You!

> King Ezechias said with tears: *"My life is cut off as by a*
> *weaver; while I was yet beginning, he cut me off."*
> —Isa.xxxviii. 12.

How many dances has he cut in on?
How many blueprints fudged.
And then there is only one set of hands,
applauding!

You do not want to see that face.

You may not see this from an arm chair!

You may not have the recipe!

The highest roller
always loses in this game, the most exalted
shiver.

And the heave of your short life's work?
What will it amount to—
that vain issue
of suspect conception?

Death will pull back the veil,
let us see the carnage.

Of what use were the honors
we never deserved

when all roads lead to a dark
bone locker? And the pompous obsequies?
What will they do
but cloak your urgency?

And who will pray for you then?

Nothing earthly holds the weight we give it;
each collapses like the lie which raised it,
smiling next to us.

> *He hath made me, says Job, as it were a byword of the*
> *people, and an example before them.*
> *—Job, xvii, 6.*

The rich man, so alive to the possibilities
of money, or the minister of state,
looking wide-eyed, like he'd just broken a rule
or something—dies,
his absence noted so quickly
that there is no time
for anyone to stop before his grave.

After burial his body will mingle, fittingly,
with the poor of the earth,
and they will have the final say.

> *The small and the great are there.*
> *—Job, iii. 19.*

Has he profited from that table, his body?
Of what use was the power he turned his way?
He is in fragments now—
where no recorder goes.

And what about his soul?
His going, neither benefiting him nor anyone else,
so swift was his passing.

To be the occasion for no reflection!
Not to have made enough money
even for his own profit!

Let us hasten to do now
what we shall not have strength or habit to do then—
that which will bring us, in the end,
neither friends, nor profit.

> *Antisthenes, though a pagan, being asked what was the
> greatest blessing which man could receive in this
> world, answered, a good death.*

> *St. Andrew Avellino said with trembling: "Who knows what
> will be my lot in the next life? Shall I be saved or damned?"*

The only fitting posture
is on our faces—always!
Guarding every thought as we would a soldier

under our command!

Send it nowhere lightly.

Worship with your eyes closed;
walk around what will kill you.
Take vengeance on me, Heavenly King,
give me a perpetual sorrow.
Mother, walk the aisle between the desks,
the trees,
set your students straight.

Consideration IV
The Certainty of Death

> *"It is appointed unto men once to die."*
> *—Hebr. ix. 27*

The chopping block,
splintered from use, could almost
be a shabby, tinted flower,
widening, as it does, at the top—
though its fragrance
will not please.

You are a man, you must die.

> *"Our other goods and evils," says Augustine, "are*
> *uncertain; death alone is certain."*

Will the chubby, blessed infant,
the one with the extra crease
in her forearm be favored,
will she have robust health,
will her years be spent
on a good earth?

No. She will die.

> *St. Augusutine says, "Fire, water, the sword, and the power*
> *of princes may be resisted; but death cannot be resisted."*

> *Belluacensis relates that at the end of his life a certain king*
> *of France said: "Behold, with all my power, I cannot induce*
> *death to wait one more hour for me."*

When the yarn is cut, the muses will leave
a second before we
and our favorite fictions do.

> *Thou hast appointed his bounds, which cannot be passed.*
> *—Job, xiv. 5.*

Appointed reader, though your life
be filled with plenty:
the squeals of children,
grass to cut on Saturdays,
these are diversions.

Each line speeds us past the date:
the black balloons,
the almost excited participants.

> *Who is the man that shall live and not see death?*
> *—Ps. lxxxviii. 49.*

What's happened to the extraordinary:
Picasso, John Paul II,
will happen to you.
The streets of Manhattan, a century ago,
are empty of high hats:
no one there now with a point of view.

Every philanthropist, too,
has since found a less captive audience.
Nothing there but marble;
no feet find time to visit any more—
no librarian applauds.

"Tell me," says Bernard, "where are the lovers of the world?
Of them nothing remains save ashes and worms."

What would it profit you
if your banquets actually fed you anyway?

How long could you eat?

Lord, I have set no blank table—
nor provided
no food!

We are born, says St. Cyprian, with the halter round our
necks; every step we take is to the grave.

Just as we have dressed
for so many silken caskets, hot-house flowers,
so others, if they can forgive
our self-lacerating strip-tease,
will stand in dressed line for us.

And how would you take a man,
on his way to the guillotine,
who delivered one-liners:
"My kingdom for a horse," or
"Cut to the dancers—the dancers"?

Your friends,
didn't they put humor aside
when death came?
Didn't they line up like little soldiers,
each silent, wise as Solomon,

under the weight
of folded hands.

> *Each of them says to you: Yesterday for me; today for thee.*
> *—Ecclus. xxxviii. 23.*

They are still with us:
in Goodwill clothes, in the silver they've left.
We wear the shirts of the dead,
drink from their cups,
walk above the ground on floors
they once paced.

Every generation
houses receive brighter coats of paint;
streets, new Christmas apparel.
And the former inhabitants?
What of them, all their promises,
stretching their wet necks as they did,
losing?

No one remembers that now.

Our laughter will end;
Death will take out his pocket watch,
the numbers falling off.

He'll smile a little before raising his head.

Neither you nor I, nor any one alive now
will live to see his youth again.

> *Days shall be formed and no one in them*
> *Ps. cxxxviii. 16.*

Only the thought of death
can keep us
where we belong.

We lapse
because the devil is a hawker,
a head turner. In baggy striped pants
he bangs his cane, flat,
on the sideshow table,
working us, rebuking
passers-by at the same time,
anything to keep us, them—
promising gain, again.

If we wish to live well,
we shouldn't.

> *O death, thy sentence is welcome.*
> *—Ecclus. xli. 3.*

> *"Consider the end of life," says St. Laurence Justinian,*
> *"and you will love nothing in this world."*

> *All that is in the world is the concupiscence of the flesh,*
> *of the eyes and the pride of life.*
> *—1 John, ii. 16.*

Illusion comes with such good will!
The sound of applause, the feel of silk.
But the saints eat at tables
which are never their own.

St. Charles Borromeo kept a skull
at his desk, so that he might have
fruitful conversation.

> *Cardinal Baronius had inscribed on his ring the words,*
> *"Remember death."*

> *The Venerable P. Juvenal Ancina, Bishop of Saluzzo, had*
> *this motto written on a skull, "What you are, I was;*
> *and what I am, you shall be."*

> *A holy hermit being asked when dying how he could be so*
> *cheerful, said: "I have always kept death before my eyes; and*
> *therefore, now that is has arrived, I see nothing new in it."*

Listen!
Earth can only be had in the passing:
our hearts are too small to hold it.

You and I *will* be there,
on that most amazing of days,
when everyone we never noticed,
the little ones, get the first praise;

when everything we did
will be made so public
that we would die of embarrassment—
if that were possible.

(It'll be the only circus—
all those little red wagons—
in town.)

Lord, take me
before You do;
I have become a mire without a name,
a tepidity.

Consideration V
Uncertainty of the Hour of Death

> *"Be you then also ready; for at what hour you think*
> *not, the Son of man will come."*
> *—Luke xii. 40.*

How could what we are—die?

I wouldn't know myself anymore.

How could there not be other lilacs?

And in the middle of our concerns,
we are told, the Ice Man cometh.

But when, and on which night?
When the moon is clouded, the cities quiet,
but our hearts not? During Mardi Gras, perhaps,
in the streets of Rio
or Steubenville?

> *The day of the Lord shall so come as a thief in the night.*
> *—I Thess. v. 2.*

He warns us to stay keen-eyed, vigilant,
to go without sleep,
to ride the fences, sloughs
of our backwater lives.

> *St. Gregory says that, for our good, God conceals from us*
> *the hour of death, that we may always be prepared to die.*

We know, we know!
The Bother, The Nuisance…waits:
Mr. Melodrama.
But really, who has time for *that* guy?
We have our lives to live, and who wants
to sit up for some whack-job,
squirting flower in his lapel.
He's a long-winded bore
if you want to know the truth,
tries to steer every conversation his way,
make each remark
depend on his hang-dog looks.
Even the most faded Floridian
in dried spittle doesn't want to see him.
We'd all prefer to sleep through it frankly,
bypass the puffed-up dread-locked
vaudevillian altogether, the only man around
with nothing better to do.

But how long do you think
you can filibuster?

And who do you think among today's dead
would have picked *this* day?

The late June sun is out—
even the grass is free.
Families put down towels at the public pool.
(Someone's brought a huge squirt gun!)
People will rent videos to watch
this summer evening with their kids.

Of all who have gone since May,
did any of them put a yellow smiley face

on this calendar day?
Did they know these high, white clouds,
the direction of this breeze?
Who of us is prophet enough for that?

We do not know how many hours we have.

We do not own that timepiece.

And how many, in the act of feasting
on one kind of dead flesh or another,
have taken their leave so quickly
that they couldn't even get a hand up
to say goodbye?

> *As fishes are taken with the hook, says Ecclesiastes,*
> *so men are taken in the evil time.*
> *—Eccles. ix. 12.*

Lord, you've pardoned me
to no good behavior.
But where else
can the hell-bent youth
I've never left far enough behind
go?

Mary!

> *Except you be converted, He will brandish His sword.*
> *—Ps. vii. 13.*

Survivors shine, their own badges.
But this world
can't reward them sufficiently,
and the next
rejects the proposition.

> *For when they shall say: Peace and security: then*
> *shall sudden destruction come upon them.*
> *—I Thess. v. 3.*

> *"He who tells you to beware," says St. Augustine,*
> *"does not wish to take away your life."*

Who can be ready?

Not you.

And so we prepare, badly:
our heads filled with half-submerged
judgments, our hearts, stale with the weight
of the nearly forgiven.

> *Delay not to be converted to the Lord, and defer it not from*
> *day to day; for His wrath shall come on a sudden, and in*
> *the time of vengeance He will destroy thee.*
> *—Eccles. v. 8.*

Sin is no man's friend.

> *"If then you must renounce it at some time, why do you not*
> *abandon it at this moment?" says St. Augustine.*

But we have trouble feeling urgent
when there are so many

sunny days to fill.
So we live the life Christ gives us—
for a limited time only—
our strides trying to inhere.

We do not know what waits for us,
but for the obstinate, if that is, here, another,
the hour of death
will be the time
that has finally come around.

What would I give for a good life?

All I have are apologies,
all I will ever have.

You have spent all Your blood on me,
and I've lost that through complacency.
I've kept myself busy testing You,
to see how far I can go and still be true,
to see how much You'll endure today.
You took me in, and I broke away.
You sought me again, but I said wait awhile,
there are flavors I have not put on file.

The End says "be prepared,"
not "prepare yourselves": as if ruin,
and not a bishop
were approaching.

> *St. Augustine says that God conceals from us the last day
> of life, that we may be always prepared to die.*

243

> *St. Paul tells us that we must work out our salvation,*
> *not only with fear, but also with trembling.*
> —*Phil. ii. 12.*

We get life, one step at a time.
Our next may well come down
on a different road.

And how many roses do we ever have with us
at any one time?

We are forever stuck
in the bald fare of the present,
whatever our plans—
without recourse
beyond a quick prayer
to remind us
of where we hope our treasure is.

> *If the tree fall to the south or to the north, in which place*
> *soever it shall fall, there shall it lie.*
> —*Eccles. xi. 3.*

If, when death intervenes,
we are found in a grace we cannot feel
or know—oh! with what delight shall we fend
with friends then! But if the end
is hard, locks down, if we are jerked out,
still paying unfelt tribute to idols…

How can we ever know
in which house we are living?

The fear of an unhappy eternity made the venerable Father Avila, apostle of Spain, say, when the news of death was brought to him: "Oh! That I had a little more time to prepare for death!"

St. Arsenius, too, trembled at the hour of death; and being asked by his disciples, why he was so much alarmed, he said: "My children this fear is not new to me; I have had it always during my whole life."

NOTES

"II. How he was imprisoned in Perugia. . ."

The two quotes in this poem come from the source material:
The Legend of The Three Companions of Saint Francis.

Bernart de Ventadorn was a rare troubadour in that he had
his start in the lower classes, among whom he worked as a
baker. Francis may have known about him, as the saint seems
to have been quite concerned with upward mobility early on
in these oral tales.

"III. The Third Consideration of the Holy Stigmata…"

Francis' mother initially named him Giovanni.

"Anna-Maria Taigi: White Noise"

"Pressing" was a torture employed by Bloody Elizabeth, who
had Catholics crushed under a door, weighted by increasing
numbers of heavy stones.

The Curé of Ars is St. John Vianney, the patron saint of par-
ish priests. He is best known for his still-available sermons, his
long confessional lines, and for his battles with the devil.

"Anna-Maria Taigi: Family"

St. Benedict Labré was a saint whose vocation was never finding one. He was a flea-bitten drifter until he died in Rome.

Anna's cause was initially delayed because the Inquisitor feared she may have been given to vanity.

"The Apprentice as Columbo"

Columbo was an absent-minded TV detective who would flail his arms around while obliquely linking up the telling evidence, all of course, to the great annoyance of his brilliant, guilty adversary, who had to stand there and take it—the show's hour almost up.

"The Apprentice Sees Himself in the Sunset"

Jimmy Swaggart, the Swag-man, was a noted TV evangelist and cousin of Jerry Lee Lewis. He was caught on several occasions with prostitutes (of the golden heart).

The flowers bring to mind the old sixties' commercial, where hippie-types, arm in arm, sang: "I'd like to buy the world a Coke, and keep it company," followed by something about "apple trees and honey bees and snow-white turtle doves."

"But what would the Apprentice/do to live there?" is a shameless lifting and variation of a line from Tom Andrews's wonderful poem, "Praying with George Herbert in late Winter."

Alan Iverson is a diminutive assassin who plays in the NBA. He is famous for his lightning-quick cross-over dribble, a move which surely confounds any still-living referee from the fifties—a time before black people and athletic creativity had been invented.

"Cleveland, December"

Ezra Pound lamented late that he could not make his Cantos cohere.

"California"

Al Luplow was one of many moderately talented outfielders who played for the Cleveland Indians during their almost half-century of distinct mediocrity. He is best remembered by many for a great leaping catch he once made, banging his knees into the top of the outfield fence, flipping over that, just his glove emerging, ball still secure.

Albert Belle, on the other hand, was a man of great talent, and rage, who played during the contemporary Indians fans' glimpse of illusion/glory: '94-'97. In 1995, he hit fifty home runs as well as fifty-two doubles, batting a robust .317.

"For Fr. Pelton, my Spiritual Director (Matthew 5: 1-5)"

A *poustinik* is a Madonna House staff person who spends about half of his or her time in hermitage and about half living in more tangible community.

**"Eleanore Holiday
(Matthew 6: 19-21)"**

Billy Holiday, the great jazz/blues singer, saw her father lynched when she was a small girl. Her subsequent signature song, "Strange Fruit," was written to help her deal with that.

**"On God, Who Writes Straight With Crooked Lines
(Matthew 7: 13-14)"**

The title for this sonnet was lifted from the talks of the Servant of God, Catherine Doherty.

About the Author

David Craig has published nine collections of poetry: *The Sandaled Foot* (Cleveland State University Poetry Center, 1980), *Psalms* (Park Bench Press, 1982), *Peter Maurin and Other Poems* (Cleveland State University Poetry Center, 1985), *Marching Through Gaul* (Scripta Humanisitica, 1990), *Only One Face* (White Eagle Coffee Store Press, 1994), *The Roof of Heaven* (Franciscan University Press, 1998), *Mercy's Face: New & Selected Poems, 1980-2000* (Franciscan University Press, 2000), *Sonnets from Matthew* (Franciscan University English Department Chapbook, 2002). His poetry has been anthologized eleven times, most significantly in David Impastato's *Upholding Mystery* for Oxford University Press, where he shared space with only twelve other Christian poets in the English-speaking world. His *Mercy's Face* was recently included in the *Masterplots* list of the five hundred most important literary works in the history of Christendom.

In 1994 David Craig co-edited (with Janet McCann) *Odd Angles of Heaven*, an anthology of contemporary Christian poetry for Harold Shaw Publishers. In 2000, Craig and McCann released an anthology of contemporary Catholic poetry from Story Line Press, entitled *Place of Passage*. In 2005 they published an historical anthology of Franciscan poems called *Poems of Francis and Clare* for St. Anthony Messenger Press.

Craig has also published three works of fiction: *The Cheese Stands Alone* (CMJ Press, 1997), *Our Lady of the Outfield* (CMJ Press, 2000), and a satirical novel, *A Communion of S(aints)* (iUniverse, 2003).

Daivd Craig has an M.F.A. and Ph.D. from Bowling Green State University. He has taught Creative Writing as a Professor at the Franciscan University of Steubenville for almost twenty years. He lives in West Virginia with his wife Linda and their three children, David Thomas, Jude Francis, and Bridget Jean.

Printed in the United States
86616LV00002B/416/A